The

MISFIT
ECONOMY

LESSONS IN CREATIVITY FROM PIRATES, HACKERS, GANGSTERS, AND OTHER INFORMAL ENTREPRENEURS

ALEXA CLAY
KYRA MAYA PHILLIPS

SIMON & SCHUSTER

NEW YORK   LONDON   TORONTO   SYDNEY   NEW DELHI

Simon & Schuster
1230 Avenue of the Americas
New York, NY 10020

First Simon & Schuster hardcover edition June 2015

SIMON & SCHUSTER and colophon are registered
trademarks of Simon & Schuster, Inc.

For information about special discounts for bulk purchases,
please contact Simon & Schuster Special Sales at
1-866-506-1949 or business@simonandschuster.com.

The Simon & Schuster Speakers Bureau can bring authors to your
live event. For more information or to book an event contact the
Simon & Schuster Speakers Bureau at 1-866-248-3049 or visit our
website at www.simonspeakers.com.

Interior design by Ruth Lee-Mui

Manufactured in the United States of America

10 9 8 7 6 5 4 3 2 1

Library of Congress Cataloging-in-Publication Data is available.

ISBN 978-1-4516-8882-5
ISBN 978-1-4516-8884-9 (ebook)

CONTENTS

Part 1

INNOVATION ON
THE FRINGE

INTRODUCTION

"AM I TALKING TOO MUCH?" SAM HOSTETLER, AN AMISH FARMER IN MILLER, Missouri, asks for the third time before continuing the story of how he, an exotic-animal aficionado, started milking camels.

Hostetler was born to devout Christian parents in Tampico, Illinois, "the same town [where] Ronald Reagan was born." When he was nine years old, his family moved to a farm in Buffalo, Missouri. His father set up a building business and became a bishop in the community church. Sam and his brothers were raised to be moral, observant, and open-minded people. He married his wife, Corlene, when he was twenty-one years old, "after knowing her forever," he says, laughing.

When Hostetler was a small child, everybody commented

on his affinity for things that lay off the beaten path. He reflects, "I don't know. I guess I've always liked a challenge." Hostetler reminisces how this love for the unusual led to his interest in exotic chickens—birds that had long tails, unlike regular chickens. When he was nine, his parents ordered twenty-five of them, and Hostetler's lifelong interest in exotic animals was born.

Hostetler's farming career began when he bought a few ostriches. He raised and traded them for a while, he said, then began to look for even more exotic animals. He bought hippos and rhinos—and became, as he likes to call it, an "alternative-livestock farmer." He has been in the trade for close to thirty years.

Then one afternoon a Missouri doctor phoned, opening the call with an unusual question: "Have you ever heard of milking camels?" Even Hostetler had never heard of such a thing in the United States. The doctor said that she wanted to give one of her patients camel milk and wondered whether Hostetler knew where she could find some. "Well, I've been known to do some crazy things over the years, one more won't hurt me," Hostetler responded.

Soon after the call, Hostetler began to plot his way into the camel milking business: a business that, to his knowledge, did not exist in the United States at the time. For Hostetler, there was some appeal in creating a new income stream, but he was drawn to the camel milking business primarily "because it was different." He started very much on a shoestring, buying a few camels, but eventually his herd grew to around thirty. He enjoys the challenge of doing something unusual, and he appears to have an affinity with the animals. He says: "I just like camels. They're not pretty, they're ugly, but I like them."

DUBBED "THE WHITE GOLD OF THE DESERT," CAMEL MILK IS SEEN BY SOME AS an almost mythical elixir. It has alleged medicinal qualities, particularly in its raw, unpasteurized form, with people the world over claiming that it has helped with symptoms of Crohn's disease, autism, diabetes, Alzheimer's, and hepatitis C. Some even profess that the milk alleviates certain symptoms of HIV/AIDS.

The milk has deep historical and religious roots. To many, it's a spiritual experience: The prophet Muhammad allegedly ordered some of his companions to drink it as a natural remedy. Used for centuries in the Middle East by nomads and Bedouins to help sustain them through the harsh desert weather, camel milk has long been praised for its healing properties. It is said that it provides more absorbable calcium than any other kind of milk, and is easier to digest, nonallergenic, and antiinflammatory. Parents of autistic children claim the milk helps their kids with their motor skills and digestive system. While beliefs about camel milk's medicinal properties are widely held, most of the evidence for its effects on disorders and diseases has been anecdotal so far.

Despite being popular in Asia, the Middle East, and Africa, the commodity has been largely ignored in the United

States. Only in the last five years has an embryonic market—a true misfit economy—started to develop, bringing together a diverse group of unlikely characters, including Amish farmers like Sam Hostetler.

THE DEMAND FOR CAMEL MILK HAS GIVEN FAMILIES LIKE HOSTETLER'S A steady, sustainable income. Other Amish and Mennonite farmers have joined him, buying camels when they become available and building small herds on their farms. We spoke to Marlin Troyer, another of the farmers to enter the trade. A Mennonite who lives and works in Branch, Michigan, Troyer told us how his entrance into the business let him grow his farm from ten to eighty acres in the span of four years. The demand for camel milk, he says, "allows my family and me to make the necessary payments to keep our farm steady and in working order."

Hostetler, too, began to experience growth in demand for camel milk, leading him to establish Humpback Dairies, a private membership association through which he sells his product. Most Amish farmers in the business sell through several permutations of this model.

Raw camel milk is sold in this way because selling raw milk (as opposed to pasteurized milk) from any source (including a cow) is illegal in many states. In all cases, it is illegal to distribute raw milk across state lines. What is legal is to consume produce from livestock that you own. So Hostetler and his family, and those who buy into his livestock by joining the Humpback

Dairies association, are allowed to consume the milk produced by the camel herd.

Most of Hostetler's business arrived through referrals, by word of mouth and family recommendations. This changed when a then-twenty-three-year-old University of Southern California graduate showed up on his doorstep.

WALID ABDUL-WAHAB, A NATIVE OF SAUDI ARABIA, ARRIVED IN THE UNITED States in 2009 to enroll in the University of Southern California's Marshall School of Business. Shortly after his graduation in September 2013, Abdul-Wahab became the first person to establish a camel milk retail business in the United States.

This venture has not been without its challenges, given the illegality of distributing raw camel milk across state lines, the outright illegality of raw milk in many states, and the small population of camels in the United States. However, with admirable determination, Abdul-Wahab has sought to navigate these obstacles and others (including constant scrutiny from the U.S. Food and Drug Administration) in the pursuit of his commercial goal.

The genesis of Desert Farms, Abdul-Wahab's company, lies in a trip he took to his home country of Saudi Arabia during his sophomore year in college. His visit coincided with the traditional Muslim holiday of Ramadan, during which observers of the religion must fast every day from dawn until sunset for one month. One evening a friend approached him with what he says was a very unappetizing dripping Ziploc bag of camel milk. "It wasn't really very attractive at the start," he says. When Abdul-Wahab asked where he got it, his friend responded that he had traveled twenty miles into the desert and picked it up from a Bedouin.

The moment Abdul-Wahab drank the milk, he fell in love with it. A couple of days later, he came up with an idea: Bring this drink to health-conscious Californians. When a class project for an entrepreneurship course came around, he began to research the state of camel milk production in the United States. He wanted to ascertain whether a market existed.

Abdul-Wahab found that it did, though in a very small way. Only a handful of people like Sam Hostetler and Marlin Troyer owned and milked camels, and as described above, they sold it solely through cooperatives. Abdul-Wahab drew a comparison with the Dallas Buyers Club, founded by Ron Woodroof and the subject of an Oscar-nominated film in 2013. Woodroof, who was suffering from AIDS, smuggled into the United States illegal pharmaceutical drugs that he had found improved his health. Wanting to sell them to others, he and a partner established the Dallas Buyers Club, which distributed the drugs to those who wished to join and pay a monthly fee.

"It didn't have to be like drugs," Abdul-Wahab told us. "People believe that camel milk helps them . . . [and] if it's helping people, we don't want to create a black market for it."

So he wrote a business plan in which he developed his aspirations to take the drink into the mainstream. He advertised in newspapers: "Have camels? Milk them!" He traveled all across the United States to find camel farmers. He met a few who had already been milking camels and selling their product through private membership associations. However, many camel owners were just leasing their camels ten weeks a year, for nativity scenes. Abdul-Wahab began to sell them on the idea that camel milk could be a new and sustainable source of income.

Abdul-Wahab struck an exclusive deal with seven Amish farmers in Colorado, Michigan, Ohio, Missouri, Pennsylvania, and Texas. Building the relationships was not an easy task. With the Amish's strong stance against technology, it was difficult to sustain communication. "A firm handshake was all I had as a guarantee of a deal," he said. Because Abdul-Wahab is Muslim, he said he could connect with the Amish on the basis of being judged by his religious beliefs. He pays the farmers for their labor and for the milk itself (eighty dollars per gallon), and provides all the machinery and supplies to milk the animals and bottle the milk.

While Abdul-Wahab spends much of his time arguing with the U.S. Food and Drug Administration—who many times have raided the camel farms he works with—he and his team ("me, the farmers, and the camels") have managed to get seventy Whole Foods stores across five states to stock pasteurized camel milk. Desert Farms also distributes raw camel milk through small mom-and-pop shops across the United States.

It was this goal—getting camel milk into Whole Foods—

that he had in the back of his mind when he started developing his business. We asked whether he feels like a success now. In his quiet yet expressive voice, he gives a resounding no. His parents were Palestinian refugees who met while hiding in an apartment during the first Lebanon war. By the time his father was twenty-four years old, he had already made his first million. His father, along with Abdul-Wahab's older brother, runs a family steel business, which supplies large government projects in Saudi Arabia. Abdul-Wahab tells us how his father jokes that he sent his son to one of America's top business schools, and yet he ended up a farmer. In a family constantly urging him to craft a career in investment banking, Abdul-Wahab feels like a misfit, constantly trying to prove the virtue of his mission.

While Abdul-Wahab hit a hundred thousand dollars of turnover six months after establishing his operation, he still hopes to make much more of a splash in the drinks industry. The market for alternatives to cow's milk (soy, almond, rice, coconut) has grown by 30 percent since 2011.[1] At the same time, the consumption of cow's milk has been in decline, from a per capita consumption of 273.8 pounds in 1970 to 198.8 in 2012.[2] Camel milk can, according to Abdul-Wahab, join the ranks of the billion-dollar American dairy alternatives industry.

SAM HOSTETLER AND WALID ABDUL-WAHAB ARE, EACH IN HIS OWN WAY, *misfits*, forging a path in the unconventional world of camel milk trading. And yet, from these misfits, we can learn much about ingenuity, about determination, about the innate human itch to create, build, and exploit an opportunity.

By definition, a misfit is "a person whose behavior or attitude sets them apart from others in an uncomfortably conspicuous way."[3] While some misfits—like Sam and Walid—are merely unconventional, many others are branded as outsiders—swindlers, rogues, scavengers, vagrants, gangsters, hackers, and hermits—and are frequently met with skepticism and suspicion. Yet across the globe, in small towns and large cities, there are misfits operating more creatively than some of the world's biggest companies, developing solutions to challenges that traditional businesses can't touch.

The characters you will read about in this book are found on pirate ships. They're found in gangs and within hacker collectives. They're in the crowded streets of Shenzhen, the prisons of Somalia, the flooded coastal towns of Thailand. Resourceful and creative, loyal and wily, they are slum dwellers, dissidents, and outlaws.

Call it the gray market, the black market, the informal economy. Or shadow markets or the makeshift economy. We call it the Misfit Economy. Whatever the term, misfit innovators inhabit a different world—a world that, by conventional wisdom, should have nothing to do with traditional businesses and mainstream markets. However, far from being deviants who pose a threat to our social and economic stability, these entrepreneurial misfits are pioneering new ways of thinking and operating, establishing new best practices that we all can learn from and apply to formal markets.

This book investigates the true stories of underground innovation and distills five key principles unique to the Misfit Economy. These stories and principles are based on our original research, which began in 2011 with a focus on social entrepreneurs and innovators in the informal economy, but soon expanded to include the black market and artistic and activist communities, as well as insider misfits working to transform some of our most established institutions. After sourcing more than five thousand case studies, we narrowed our selection to a top thirty that we decided to explore in more depth.

Our aim was to bring attention to misfits operating within diverse geographies across the globe, fields of practice (the arts, technology, activism, black and informal markets), and time periods (we sought out stories of both contemporary and historic misfits). In addition to diversity, the top thirty cases had to meet criteria of originality. These misfits had to pioneer an unusual, creative, or alternative way of working. They had to be innovating. And that innovation had to lead to some kind of disruption—to the transformation of an attitude, norm, or organizational practice.

The more we probed these misfit economies, the more we learned that the underground and informal economies can be plagued by the same level of conformity one finds in the mainstream economy. Working for a Mexican drug cartel can be a lot like working for Exxon: You are subjected to a hierarchical command-and-control system. That's why the innovation angle became our knockout test for selecting the stories in this book. To make the cut, these misfits couldn't be just outsiders; they had to be innovative and disruptive outsiders.

TAKE SOMALI PIRATES. THEIR STORY IS NOT JUST ONE OF THEFT, IT IS A STORY of transformation: from a small, local, and informal industry to a large, international, and sophisticated business that has not only appeared in media across the world but also driven the development of a counter-piracy industry. It is also a story of opportunity or, rather, a story of how you build a market opportunity where one does not seem to exist.

Piracy first arose in Somalia in the early 1990s, as a response to foreign ships illegally fishing in Somalia's waters. The country had recently experienced a collapse of its government, and its navy and coastal police were unable to effectively repel this illegal fishing. Faced with diminished fishing stocks, an economy in turmoil, and an inability to find alternative employment, some fishermen turned to attacking foreign fishing vessels.

In these early days, piracy in Somalia was a relatively informal and unsophisticated business. A former pirate whom we spoke to, Abdi (no surname given), attested to this. He told us that he and his friends attacked foreign trawlers in their fishing skiffs in Hafun, a coastal town in northeastern Somalia. Abdi built the group with friends and family from his clan, splitting the spoils according to how much each person invested.

These original pirates—the aggrieved fishermen—were, in essence, hustlers. They had noticed that valuable cargo was crossing their shores; struggling with low fishing stock, they spotted a chance to gain income in a different, albeit illegal, way. Their country was in economic and social disarray, their livelihoods threatened by the foreign trawlers illegally encroaching on their waters.

Instead of accepting this destiny, these individuals took matters into their own hands. They did not sit back and wait for the government to improve things. They did not just continue to fish with ever-decreasing success. Rather, they recognized an opportunity and seized it. They had limited resources—just an idea and fishing boats—but driven by scarcity and the desire for income, they sowed the seeds of what would evolve into a lucrative and sophisticated criminal movement.

From its informal beginning, piracy in Somalia evolved rapidly, gaining major international attention in 2008 with the capture of the Ukrainian ship MV *Faina*. The ship, which was carrying military cargo—grenade launchers and tanks—was released by the pirates after they received $3.5 million in ransom money. The operation was a professional one and an illustration of how piracy in Somalia would develop.

The MV *Faina* was hijacked by a group of pirates led by a man who goes by the name of Afweyne (which translates to "Big Mouth"). Afweyne had founded the Somali Marines—a group of highly trained pirates—after searching and finding investors to turn what was an opportunistic, disorganized operation into a functioning, plan-driven business. Afweyne's group was well organized, working very much as a military operation would, with a leadership hierarchy delineating admirals, vice admirals, and lieutenants.

Many credit Afweyne with being one of the key figures responsible for transforming Somali piracy from a scrappy, self-funded force into a well-invested, transnational multimillion-dollar industry. The spoils of piracy would soon after be traced as far as India and Dubai, with ransom money reinvested in equipment and training but also put toward the development of the khat drug trade (khat is a narcotic plant popular in Somalia).

For pirates such as Afweyne, the use of mother ships (usually fishing dhows) distinguished their attacks from those of the less sophisticated, earlier generations of a pirate mission. Setting their base in the ocean via these mother ships, rather than on the shore, allowed the professional groups to extend their reach into the high seas, way beyond local waters, enabling them to target bigger cargo ships.

Some pirates we spoke with told us how, using these mother ships, they would head out to shipping lanes, waiting to spot a vessel, and then launch an opportunistic attack with a two-, sometimes three-skiff team. Once the pirates take control of the ship, they steer it to shore, where a negotiator engages with the shipping company and others to agree on a ransom payment. While the negotiation is ongoing, a local economy serves the hostages and the pirates, providing them with food, water, and khat. Pirate gangs also employ lawyers, pimps to service gangs with prostitutes, and banknote checkers who use machines to detect fake money.

Another pirate whom we spoke with, Abdi Hasan, described a similar strategy of attack, speaking of an operation that was even more organized. Unlike the pirate crews who would simply head out to shipping lanes, waiting to launch an opportunistic attack on a passing vessel, his organization had been guided by someone who resides abroad—"probably Dubai," our fixer interjected—who would provide the location of the suitable target ship. He and others spoke of how pirates tended to target slower and undermanned ships that had low freeboards (for easier boarding); and they preferred to attack at dusk, when visibility was low. Hasan told us that he and other foot soldiers would get paid regardless of the result of the attack: if the ship was captured and a ransom was appropriated, the pirates received higher compensation; if it wasn't, less.

It has been reported that in the case of a successful mission, pirates receive between $30,000 and $75,000 each, and that the first pirate to board a ship—and those who bring their own weapon or ladder—receive a $10,000 bonus.[4] They can chew khat and eat and drink on credit, which is then deducted from their share of the ransom when it is received. These sorts of operations may require $30,000 of financing, usually provided by fishermen, former pirates, ex-police and military officials, and khat dealers, who take between 30 and 75 percent of the spoils.[5]

This difference in strategy—from waiting and attacking a passing target to knowing exactly where it sits and then heading out—is reflective of the shift in business model: from a local cottage industry to a commercial business with international support, driven by a group of innovators (the business leaders, the financiers, the pirates themselves) who were able to adapt their business according to its potential for growth.

Somali piracy seeped its way into international attention because its successes were frequent, far-reaching (well beyond Somalia's territorial waters), and lucrative. A November 2013 report by the World Bank, Interpol, and the United Nations stated that, since the first known hijacking in April 2005, up to $385 million U.S. had been claimed as ransom money for 179 hijacked ships.

The phenomenon has also increased the cost of trade, causing an estimated $18 billion U.S. expense to the world economy. International navies have naturally ramped up their presence in the region in an attempt to thwart the threat, though pirates have been innovative in their responses to greater and more concerted efforts to catch them. Each pirate we spoke to told how they upgraded to faster skiffs, improved their methods of communication—stocking up on satellite phones—and carried heavier weaponry to break through safety rooms in ships.

WHILE SOMALI PIRATES HAVE GAINED WIDESPREAD INTERNATIONAL ATTENtion, many misfits—such as smugglers, waste pickers, or camel milk traders—are under the radar, operating in the shadows with great stealth. They represent the ingenuity of the underground. And so this book asks: Who are these unknown hustlers? How do they work? How do they organize themselves? How do they catalyze innovation? What challenges do they face? And—most important—what can we learn from them?

A caveat before we continue: While there is undoubtedly a dark side to some of the innovation, this book is not intended as an endorsement of criminal activity. We are aware that arms traders deliver weapons that fuel genocides. Drug cartels encourage debilitating addiction. Human traffickers continue to maintain reprehensible slave and sex trade across the globe. We are not attempting to glorify the immorality of these actions.

Rather, the argument we make is simple: The free market economy does not possess a monopoly on innovation. While many great innovation practices have been and will be distilled from the Googles, eBays, and Toyotas of the world, our research has revealed that not only has underground innovation been overlooked as a significant driver of the economy, but it also offers its own unique and valuable insights.

While other innovation-related books rightly chronicle the creativity and ingenuity of fast-moving start-ups, corporate strategy, and visionary CEOs, this book goes outside the conventional scope to show a broader view of the world economy. Formal markets are only one part of the whole. We will make visible some portion of the rest.

Chapter 1

THE MISFIT PHILOSOPHY

URBAN EXPERIMENT (THE UX), A CLANDESTINE HACKER GROUP WE MET IN France, has a mission to undertake positive collective experiments. Some of its members, among other activities, spend a lot of their time using the unauthorized sections of the underground tunnel system in Paris to break into buildings and restore national artifacts that have, in their opinion, been neglected by the traditional institutions of the French state. Known as the Untergunther, this subgroup of the UX is infamous for breaking into the Panthéon in Paris repeatedly over a year to restore a neglected nineteenth-century clock, much to the chagrin of French authorities. Author and journalist Jon Lackman asked them: "Why do you do it?" Lazar Kunstmann, the group's spokesperson, responded with a simple question:

"Do you have plants in your home? Do you water them every day?" For the UX, fixing is second nature. They see themselves as fulfilling a higher duty to "take care of the forgotten artifacts of French civilization."[1]

Why break in? you may wonder. Why not forge a legitimate business providing these services? When we spoke to Kunstmann, it became clear to us that the UX works faster, leaner, and in a more focused way than any of the bureaucratic institutions charged with the care and preservation of these artifacts of French history and culture. The UX feels a responsibility for preserving them. So they make it happen, on their own terms.

THE UX IS A BAND OF MISFITS. THEY SHAKE THINGS UP—THEY QUESTION AUthority, provoke, and experiment.

Who are the other misfits around us?

They are the rogues who threaten the stability of business as usual. The renegades who work against the grain of their organization or community. The nonconformists who are more excited by ambiguity, uncertainty, and possibility than reality. The rebels who break the rules and challenge the perspectives of others. The eccentrics who wrestle with their deepest motivations, embracing their own oddities. The mavericks who aren't afraid to build on others' ideas and freely share their own, no matter how utopian or far-fetched.

• • •

BORN IN 1887, BRITISH DOCTOR HELENA WRIGHT BROKE BARRIERS AS A woman entering the medical profession and was an early advocate for sex education and family planning services, as well as a key matchmaker in helping to broker adoptions.[2] While adoption today is a mainstream practice (and a $13 billion industry in the United States), Wright was a pioneer of the service. Through her clinics, she matched women seeking abortions or unable to care for their offspring with women in want of children. Wright was a radical figure at the time, challenging societal modesty by offering contraception and sex education for the purposes of family planning.

Wright went on to help form the National Birth Control Association and the International Committee on Planned Parenthood. In her book *Sex and Society* (1968), she argued that individuals should develop their sexual expression beyond parenthood. She was a pioneer of the "sex positive" attitude, arguing that sex shouldn't be regarded with guilt or as a "dirty" act.

In her personal life, Wright was also a bit of a misfit, participating in an open marriage, carrying out séances from her home, and holding interests in astrology and life after death. She believed that today's cranks were tomorrow's prophets and faced opposition throughout her career from the medical establishment, social workers, and a legal system that struggled to keep up with her innovations.

Misfits such as Helena Wright display remarkable ingenuity in solving problems many are afraid to touch, let alone acknowledge. Misfits fundamentally challenge the established practices of incumbent institutions, pushing boundaries and exploring opportunities that others might be too risk-averse or traditional to pursue. They provoke new mind-sets and attitudes, catalyzing big societal conversations about issues like sexuality, violence, human rights, equality, and education. True misfits don't just seek to provide a substitution for an existing service; they question whether the service is necessary in the first place.

Take the education industry, where misfit disrupters have, rather than proposing alternatives to four-year college or university, questioned the basis for formal schooling altogether (through the unschooling movement) and sought to radically transform the practice of learning itself.

In her book *Don't Go Back to School*, independent learning advocate Kio Stark profiles a number of misfits who have found alternatives to formal education. In Stark's words, "My goal was the opposite of reform . . . not about fixing school [but] about transforming learning—and making traditional school one among many options rather than the only option." Stark dropped out of her Ph.D. program because she found it too constricting. She writes, "People who forgo school build their own infrastructures. They borrow and reinvent the best that formal schooling has to offer."

Another misfit education innovator, Dale Stephens, founded UnCollege, which aims to offer curricula for self-directed learning. Stephens dropped out of school when he was twelve. He decided that rather than be taught by teachers in classrooms, he would seek out mentors who could teach him what he wanted to learn. Today, thanks in part to misfits such as Stark and Stephens, alternative education is fast becoming a growing marketplace, with online platforms like Skillshare and Coursera providing alternatives to traditional degrees. Mattan Griffel, a former instructor on Skillshare and now a founder of his own start-up, One Month, taught himself code and wanted to make the learning process easier and more intuitive for others.

These instincts are also at work in health care. We spoke to Stephen Friend, who has developed a novel way of working with disease-related research, fighting the current traditionally reward-based, closed academic approach.[3] Through his non-profit Sage Bionetworks, he built a community of genomic and biomedical scientists committed to sharing ways to find treatments and cures. The pharmaceutical company Merck was one of the first to contribute clinical and genomic data that cost them $100 million to develop. Friend is working to convince more pharmaceutical companies to donate pre-competitive data. He has raised mixed funding from government, industry, and foundations. Top laboratories from academic institutions including Columbia; Stanford; the University of California, San Francisco; and the University of California, San Diego, are also participating.

Rather than working to protect their data and ideas, Friend is convincing researchers to collaborate and build upon one another's advances in the field. Launched in 2009, Sage Bionetworks lives online as an open repository of data and models, which Friend hopes will become a sort of Wikipedia for life sciences. Friend isn't just offering a new service. He is transforming research and development.

WHAT MOTIVATES A MISFIT?

The pursuit of reputation and esteem is one of the primary motivators underscoring all economic life. It is what Adam Smith termed the "impartial spectator," which drives us to act in order to accrue the esteem of others. And it is a force that is just as powerful in the black markets as in the formal economy.

Those in the mainstream feel good about themselves when others approve of or acknowledge their work, often with bonuses, raises, and promotions. Misfits aren't entirely dissimilar; many do care about their reputations. Graffiti artists try to impress one another by tagging risky locations. Hackers are constantly showing off their skills and commitment, posting their victories online for others to see. An Occupy Wall Street protestor may be just as interested in branding himself as an agitator and seeking out recognition from the community of protestors as he is in societal transformation. In fact, even within the Occupy movement, there was a certain status hierarchy at play. Those who had been with the movement since the beginning were known as "Day 1 occupiers." Protestors earned kudos from their peers based on how long they had been associated with the movement, whether they had slept in the park, and whether they had been arrested. While it may not be an MBA from Harvard Business School, misfit innovation runs on the social currency that one can receive only from peers.

The prospect of financial gain is another of the great motivating forces in the formal economy. So it is, too, in the Misfit Economy, where such gain frequently comes with recognition and respect. One innovator we met made over two thousand dollars a day selling drugs. He said he pursued that life because it brought him street cred and financial security: "I was respected among my peers and even among the grown men in my neighborhood. At the age of nineteen, I had a nice car, a beautiful apartment, and no financial worries."

Some of the other misfits profiled in this book aren't so driven by the pursuit of money. Many of the characters we encountered are motivated by creative expression, the need to fix a problem, the steady mastery of a craft or skill, the urge to protect and defend their communities, or the thrill of getting away with something. Many a misfit would agree with artist and writer Kahlil Gibran, who said, "They deem me mad because I will not sell my days for gold; and I deem them mad because they think my days have a price."

These words offer insight into a kind of double consciousness—to borrow a phrase from W. E. B. DuBois—experienced by most misfits. Most have an acute sense of "us" and "them." They are able to understand, parrot, and tap into the values of the formal system when needed, but also maintain a separate awareness.

While it may be counterintuitive, there are often altruistic motivations and justifications at work in the Misfit Economy.

Speaking to author and activist Andrew Feinstein, we learned that even arms dealers sometimes believe they are supporting the underdog or empowering the oppressed by delivering a social benefit. Feinstein told us that it wouldn't be out of character for an arms dealer to think, "I'm arming the powerless to bring peace." The con artist also possesses a twisted morality. One identity fraudster we spoke with made it clear that he would never go after someone he thought "couldn't take the hit."

In other cases, the motivations of misfit innovators are much more straightforward: They center on survival, as well as the need to protect and defend family, friends, community, or one's livelihood.

ONE OF THE FORMER SOMALI PIRATES WE SPOKE WITH, ABDI HASAN, IS A thirty-three-year-old man from Galkayo, a city in north central Somalia. Today he resides in Hargeisa Prison, an institution situated in Somaliland (an enclave that became independent of Somalia in 1991) that houses pirates convicted of hijacking ships off the Horn of Africa.

Hasan decided to become a pirate one night after returning home from his job at a hotel in Galkayo. He was then twenty-eight. "I was an orphan boy," he told us in broken but intelligible English. His parents perished during the Somali civil war, and as the oldest, he was left to support his six younger siblings. Day in and day out in his work at the hotel, he told us, he had observed pirates enjoying higher incomes, allowing them to buy houses for their families, purchase cars, and sustain their khat-chewing habit. Hungry and desperate to provide a better life for his family, he decided to join a pirate gang.

Hasan was a foot soldier throughout his piracy career, boarding and guarding the ships that were targeted and then attacked for ransom. His life as a pirate spanned five years, during which he participated in eight missions, two of which resulted in the successful receipt of ransom money. He was captured—after unsuccessfully attempting escape—by a European Union Naval Force Somalia fleet, also known as Operation Atalanta.

We asked Hasan what it was like to be a pirate. "It was terrible," he responded. He elaborated, telling us that it was traumatic to see people on the hijacked ships crying, wondering whether they would live or die. "Do you feel guilty?" we asked. He said, "Absolutely. But I was hungry." He continued to explain, via our Somali interpreter, that the hunger surpassed the guilt.

While Abdi Hasan spoke of the need to provide for his family, other former pirates indicated that the lines can blur between financial gain on the one hand and the desire to defend and support their community on the other.

In these conversations, two factors were cited repeatedly for the origin of piracy in Somalia: the lack of sustainable employment and a history of foreign encroachment on Somali fishing stock.

The Somali government's collapse in 1991 had turned the country into a fragile state unable to ensure the security, health, and prosperity of the majority of its inhabitants. Simultaneously, its navy and coastal policing bodies crumbled, meaning that fishermen working along the Somali coast lost protection from foreign ships illegally fishing in Somalia's waters. Unable to find alternative employment, some fishermen turned to attacking foreign fishing vessels along the Gulf of Aden, which forms part of the Suez Canal waterway, linking the Mediterranean to the Indian Ocean.

This narrative—the poor, unemployed, distressed fisherman who is merely taking back what was illegally taken from him—is a strong one. While the lure of money was and continues to be the primary reason Somalis turn to piracy, this story breathes life into the movement and provides an appealing rationalization for engaging in illegal and often violent behavior.

We spoke to Jay Bahadur, an author (*The Pirates of Somalia: Inside Their Hidden World*) and journalist who has spent a significant amount of time in Somalia. He told us that Somali piracy in the mid-1990s was indeed primarily a business of ex-fishermen and others attacking foreign trawlers that stayed close to Somali shores. The movement's early leaders, Bahadur said, were being genuine about the fact that they felt their fishing waters were being encroached. To them, this was a redemption movement whereby they were applying fines to illegal activity. These initial gangs then started teaching the methods to other people, and the movement spread throughout Somalia.

However, since those early days, most of Somalia's pirates have lacked a history in fishing. Fishing is a marginal activity in Somalia; it isn't traditionally Somali, and according to Bahadur, it is looked down upon by many Somalis as a way of making a living. This story, then, is presented to journalists and authors by many pirates as a way to justify their behavior. "Beyond a few aggrieved fishermen in the early days," Bahadur told us, "it doesn't really hold true."

Piracy in Somalia really took off in early 2008, when the government of Puntland experienced a collapse of sorts. Unable to pay its soldiers, the country experienced a surplus of young, armed, and unemployed men. They joined pirate gangs as a way to earn income. The Puntland coast guard even trained some of the early pirates in how to conduct boarding operations and navigate. It was this combination—a semi-collapsed government, coupled with a high monetary incentive, low risk, and the geographical location of Puntland (straddling the Gulf of Aden and the Indian Ocean)—that can be considered the catalyst for the explosion of the piracy movement in Somalia.

One pirate we spoke with, Mohamed Omar—who practiced in Eyl, a city in the autonomous state of Puntland—told of his motivations for becoming a pirate. "We didn't intend to kill anyone," he said, sitting in a Somali prison cell. "We were just poor fishermen who were attacked. We had to defend ourselves." Though when we asked him what he liked about being a pirate, he answered immediately: "The money." He added that if he fails to find employment once he is released from prison, he will return to piracy.

Abdu Said, a pirate from Hobyo, a port city in north central

Somalia, struck a similar tone: "I became a pirate so that I could save the Somali coast." After a brief pause, he added, "And to make money," trying hard to make the latter sound more like an afterthought and not a primary motivation.

BUT ISN'T "MISFIT" JUST ANOTHER WORD FOR "ENTREPRENEUR"?

While misfits and entrepreneurs share some traits—they are natural risk takers who pursue freedom and autonomy through their own passion and hustle—they shouldn't be conflated. Misfits are countercultural, self-questioning, and vulnerable. They push boundaries. They challenge systems. Sure, sometimes the misfit personality finds herself in the body of an entrepreneur, and when these identities merge, the results can be explosive.

Two businessmen in possession of this hybrid DNA are Steve Jobs and Richard Branson. Self-confident, achievement-oriented, and invested in winning over others, Jobs was a quintessential entrepreneur. He succeeded in creating one of the planet's most successful companies, bringing iconic products to the masses. And while at times Jobs seemed invincible, he wasn't afraid to show his vulnerability (a key example being his famous Stanford commencement address, in which he spoke about feeling like a failure after he was fired from his own company).

The alternative, renegade spirit he encouraged at Apple from the get-go, when the computer industry was ruled by the big buttoned-down organizations, was showcased in an infamous ad celebrating none other than the misfit:

Here's to the crazy ones. The misfits. The rebels. The troublemakers. The round pegs in the square holes. The ones who see things differently. They're not fond of rules. And they have no respect for the status quo. You can quote them, disagree with them, glorify or vilify them. About the only thing you can't do is ignore them. Because they change things. They push the human race forward. And while some may see them as the crazy ones, we see genius. Because the people who are crazy enough to think they can change the world are the ones who do.

Similarly, Richard Branson's maverick blend of entrepreneur and misfit influenced him to pursue opportunities and take risks where others were too afraid. A struggling student, perhaps due to his dyslexia, Branson founded his first entrepreneurial venture at sixteen with a magazine called *Student*, a national magazine run by and aimed at high school students. He then founded a record store, Virgin, in the crypt of a church. By the seventies, he had enough money to launch his own label and started Virgin Records. He went on to sign experimental bands such as Faust and Culture Club, whom many in the music industry were reluctant to take on.

Since the runaway success of the Virgin brand as a whole, Branson has pioneered other markets, such as space tourism, against the wisdom of many well-established friends and competitors. Branson's powerful blend of renegade entrepreneurship has made him the eighth richest citizen of the United Kingdom at the time of writing,[4] as well as an honorable member of the Misfit Economy.

Many creatives and artists we spoke with are also developing a more entrepreneurial mind-set. American filmmaker and storyteller Lance Weiler, like Branson, is dyslexic. He suffered from a speech impediment as a kid and was constantly threatened with being held back in school. He didn't go to college but instead became a film runner, running film from a movie set to the lab while sleeping in his car. He worked his way up through the industry and in 1996 got an unlikely break with his film *The Last Broadcast*, the first feature movie that you could watch on a laptop. Weiler made the movie with a friend for $900, and it ended up grossing close to $5 million.

"At the time," Weiler told us, "people thought we were bastardizing the filmmaking process because we were using digital. We weren't considered to be filmmakers." He suggested that a certain naïveté, rebelliousness, and experimentalism were key to the movie's success. "We were rebelling against a system that was permission-based." Weiler believed he was helping to define a new type of moviemaking. "We were like that little fat girl from Ohio that Francis Coppola talked about in *Hearts of Darkness*," Weiler told us. "You know, this idea that the next Mozart or beautiful film would come from some small town by a kid using their father's camera recorder. That was what we were doing."

Part of Weiler's success was due to his ability to work the system. He wrote letters to major production companies telling them he wanted to make the first digital motion picture. After he didn't hear back, he took a page from a con man's handbook and wrote the same letters but intentionally misaddressed them so they were sent to the wrong companies. Sony, for example, would get a letter intended for Barco. Within three days, he had received countless calls from these companies and offers of a free projector that he could use for the next few years. Weiler then brought digital projection to Cannes and Sundance.

When it came to releasing the movie into multiple theaters, Weiler thought about using satellite technology to beam the movie in. But he didn't know anything about satellite. He was on the phone with one satellite provider when they repeatedly asked him what competitor he was talking to. Weiler wasn't speaking to anyone else, but every time they asked, he avoided the question. Finally, he told them that if they asked one more time, he would have to end the conversation. The conversation continued, and five minutes later, they asked again. Weiler hung up the phone. His producer called him in a panic. "She thought I was crazy," he told us. The company ended up giving Weiler $2.5 million of R&D technology, far more than he'd anticipated. "I had nothing to lose. It was just this renegade spirit."

Weiler believes that an entrepreneurial mind-set is essential for any artist. "There is this myth out there that artists are a special, almost holy type of human—that because they are creative, they can't be worried or bothered by the things that take them away from that creative pursuit. There's a certain purity there." For Weiler, his big epiphany was when he realized he could be creative across all of it. Not just in the art product but in the financing, distribution, and business aspects of artistic production.

"As an artist, you have to think about the sustainability of what you're doing from an entrepreneurial standpoint—you can't ride on your sheer creative skills or 'genius.' Those days are gone, if they ever really existed," Weiler told us.

Jobs, Branson, and Weiler may be outliers. Many of the misfits we spoke with found even the path of traditional entrepreneurship too conformist. Countless misfit communities we spoke to—from hacker collectives to do-it-yourself maker networks to festival cultures—run on a more radical spirit of informality and self-governance.

THE LIFEBLOOD OF MISFITS: INFORMALITY AND SELF-GOVERNANCE

After the flooding in Thailand in early 2013 ravaged the lives of millions, Thai misfits took matters into their own hands in an example of extraordinary inventiveness.[5] The Tumblr blog Thai Flood Hacks cataloged do-it-yourself (DIY) mobility solutions for navigating flooded areas. On the blog, you could find everything from life rafts made buoyant with recycled water bottles, to abnormally stretched elevated bicycles, to homemade motorized Jet Skis. No one sought permission. It was simply done and then shared on a blog so that others could benefit from it as well.

This is a perfect example of misfit innovation. If such individuals can come up with an impromptu life-or-death solution, what could you do with fewer rules and a little more creative license?

Informality is a key driver of misfit innovation. Removing what strikes most of us as arbitrary, informality is ultimately about supporting people to rise above a job title and giving them permission to unleash their real talents. Informality is about enabling spontaneity, freeing people to depend on intrinsic motivation (their values) and instincts rather than deferring to the rules, codes, and incentives (raises and promotions) imposed by external authorities.

Informality has been a key animating force in the social movements of the past, unlocking citizen power in uprisings such as Occupy Wall Street and the Arab Spring. Moreover, this disruptive spirit is trickling into business. The increasing need for disorganization within our institutions is a trend the *Economist* highlighted in a piece entitled "In Praise of Misfits,"[6] which argues that companies are gradually coming to replace "the organization man with disorganization man.... Well-balanced executives that were the staple of many companies of the past are now being passed over for more disruptive entrepreneurs, geeks, and creatives." These types of individuals bring to the workplace decivilizing tendencies that are essential to cultivating innovation and improving the day-to-day quality of work life.

People with attention deficit disorder (ADD), the piece relays, aren't able to focus, jump from project to project, and sometimes don't finish what they start. Because of this, though, they're often fountains of new ideas. Bored easily, they conjure up new possibilities and scenarios. In contrast, employees with Asperger's syndrome have intense obsessions with repetitive tasks, patterns, numbers, and detail—all qualities that serve a computer programmer quite well. In March 2014, the *Wall Street Journal* reported[7] on the efforts of a German software company (SAP) to hire people with autism disorders, placing these employees in technical roles such as computer programming, debugging, and IT due to their ability to focus on the details.

In concert with informality, the twin thread running throughout the principles that follow is self-governance—having the right to control one's *self* versus being controlled by a top-down organization. A 2012 report on corporate behavior found that only 3 percent of more than 35,000 employees surveyed reported high levels of self-governing behavior (independence, autonomy) in their organizations.[8]

Old-school pirates developed democratic codes to govern their ships. Protestors depend on consensus building and cooperative structures of organization. Open-source communities create their own internal rules of conduct and participation. What these groups know all too well is that autonomy enables trust, commitment, and the emergence of a collective mission and purpose. The loyalty, engagement, and sense of community you find on pirate ships, among hacker communities, and running through protest movements and inner-city slums are impressive, and that is precisely because of the self-governing nature of these informal organizations. Hackers, for example, have rules, norms, and etiquette governing behavior that they enforce on a peer-to-peer level. Linux, today's most prominent example of open-source software, is driven by a peer-to-peer exchange of skills, ideas, and norms. The software—today used by more than eighteen million people—was initiated by its leader, Linus Torvalds, but was shaped by thousands of responses from all around the globe. At the time of writing, it continues to be improved on by an estimated eight thousand programmers. When improvements are submitted by regular programmers, they are received as if Torvalds had suggested them, the working motto being "Let the code decide."[9]

Misfits often embrace self-governance because they are distrustful of authority and not easily coerced into someone else's logic or command. Misfit innovators may be their own bosses or operate in networks or communities where they feel they have the ability to help shape the rules they live by. Some open-source and hacker communities have become experts at creating their own operating principles. For example, the original hackers, the group of misfits at the Massachusetts Institute of Technology, organically developed what is known as the Hacker Ethic, a code according to which they would operate:

the importance of free access to computers, freedom of information, decentralization, and judgment based solely on merit. Every hacker we spoke to gave a nod to these principles, stating that they still animate many of the hacker movements today.

WHY MISFITS ARE NEEDED NOW MORE THAN EVER

Many of the principles we see operating in the Misfit Economy have emerged in direct opposition to the legacy of formalization born of the Industrial Revolution some two hundred and fifty years ago.

The Industrial Revolution brought with it an economic logic built around efficiency, standardization, and specialization. Systems from agriculture to textile manufacturing became increasingly formalized. In turn, a demand for a labor force capable of plugging into these systems was born. Conformity (among workers) and productivity were prized; the "civilizing virtues" of industry, discipline, moderation, and obedience to authority were the gold standard. Those who didn't fit this pattern were accused of sloth, indolence, idleness, uncontrolled appetites, and excessive passions.

As economic historians have argued, industrial work allowed workers to be more effective and efficient at a given task, and to increase output and productivity. People developed mastery; on factory assembly lines, the woman who installed the nut on a specific bolt did so with confidence, ease, and precision. She also did it quicker than anyone else.

But times have changed. Most of us in the developed world aren't working on assembly lines, and the same standardization that promised mastery and efficiency doesn't apply anymore.

Steve Mariotti, founder of the Network for Teaching Entrepreneurship (NFTE), told us, "I grew up in the outskirts of Detroit. In class, they used to have a General Motors org chart on the wall. If you were bad, the teacher used to point and tell you you'd be at the bottom of the org chart—on the assembly line. Good and bad—we all knew where we were going. The education system was built for our absorption into the automobile industry."

Today there is no such linear trajectory. We are in a time of escalating change and of mass economic transition. The mortality rate of large corporations is increasing. The average life span of leading American companies has declined by over fifty years in the last hundred years: from sixty-seven years in the 1920s to only fifteen in 2012.[10] Apart from the auto sector, many other blue-chip industries are in decline. The pharmaceutical industry had its heyday in the eighties and nineties, with blockbuster drugs like Lipitor, Plavix, and Zoloft. Some in the industry have faced competition from generics and been forced to slash internal R&D.

If we listened to Joseph Schumpeter, the economist and political scientist, we'd allow the forces of "creative destruction"—the process of destroying an old economic order and the emergence of a new one—to have their way.

• • •

DAVID BERDISH IS A DEVOUT CATHOLIC AND A THIRD-GENERATION AUTO-
worker at Ford Motor Company. He worked at the company
for thirty-one years before recently retiring. His grandfather,
a prominent labor organizer and founding member of UAW
Local 600, a union that represented the largest Ford plants,
was at the infamous Battle of the Overpass, where United Auto
Worker union organizers were beaten by Ford henchmen.
Like his grandfather, David Berdish is a misfit. "I get in trouble
a lot [at Ford]. I push the boundaries of what I'm allowed to
do," he told us.

Berdish was originally hired to work at Ford Aerospace
but couldn't get security clearance because of his grandfather's
labor history. So he went on to work at Ford, first in manufacturing, then as a financial analyst, a purchasing manager,
a buyer, and a supply chain manager, before moving over to
manage Ford's sustainability practice in 2000. "It was during
my manufacturing rotations that I started understanding people and the health and safety issues." He brought his breadth
of experience within the company to start building out Ford's
leadership on human rights—health and safety—around the
world. He made sure that basic worker conditions were com-
pliant and began addressing the company's corporate responsibility commitments.

Berdish also focused on issues of access to transport. In
2007 he started working within the company on mobility solutions and urban transport options beyond cars. "The idea that
we are going to create a middle class in BRIC economies doesn't
make sense. Not everyone wants or should have 2.2 cars." In

the future, Berdish imagines a world where cars are more of a shared resource and more functional. "Cars will have to be more stripped down. In a sharing economy or mega-city, you don't need satellite radio and fancy navigation systems; you just need cars to serve a function."

Berdish helped develop mobility solutions at Ford, which meant showing the company the value of business models built around car sharing and mass urban transport options like rail, metro, buses, and bicycles. He encountered a lot of frustration, as the focus of the company was still on cars and trucks, but his vice president at the time offered support. "She really turned me loose," he told us. "She let me be a misfit and carve out some exciting opportunities for us." Part of Berdish's success owed to some protection he found in William Clay "Bill" Ford, Jr., Henry Ford's great-grandson and the executive chairman of the company. "Bill was my biggest champion. Without him, I wouldn't have taken some of the risks I took inside the company." But Bill Ford warned Berdish that there was no way he would get promoted or recognized by the system. Because Ford answers primarily to shareholders and "the company is getting analyzed day by day by Wall Street analysts," his work, which focused more on a long-term value proposition, didn't get a lot of acknowledgment or recognition internally. "That's why I was so dependent on others who could help champion my work and offer protection," Berdish explained.

While some within the company still find Berdish's message of looking beyond car manufacturing threatening, others are waking up to its reality. Across the United States, automobile consumption has peaked; it has also begun to plateau across many developed countries. Berdish's own twenty-year-old son doesn't have his driver's license. "He is more concerned with what he is downloading on his iPod," Berdish told us.

Though Berdish was a misfit, provoking his colleagues with the question of whether Ford's future should be about automobile manufacturing, he has tremendous loyalty to the company. "At Ford, I could get things done at scale and have more influence than if I worked on my own. Let's face it, Ford has more leverage and visibility than David Berdish does."

Like his grandfather, Berdish walked the line of being radical and agitating while also remaining loyal and committed. "My grandfather criticized Ford, but he didn't like anyone else to. He was really loyal and worked hard. He was just trying to get better health and safety practices into place." Similarly, Berdish gets upset with people who "blame the system" or show a lack of dedication. "If you choose to work for a company, do a high-quality job and give an honest day's work. If you are creative and passionate, you can find a way to add value and meaning to what you do."

Berdish understands the alienation and disenchantment felt by a lot of the workforce. "People get upset that they are just a number, that they are a cog in the machine. It makes sense. Some of the most incompetent people in any company are in HR. The standards and rules for promotion are pretty arbitrary. It's a lot of politics." Berdish also feels that the gap between the pay of the CEO and the lowest-paid worker is frustrating and unjust. Even though he has some criticism, he never "bitched." He had a more practical attitude. "If you want to do something different, then do it."

Reflecting on his time at Ford, Berdish told us that he is proud of what he accomplished. He believes he took a harder path within the company, the road less traveled, but didn't shy away from the challenge; like a true misfit, he is proud of the people he pissed off. When we asked him whether he thought Ford's future would depend on misfits like him, he answered, "Absolutely. I think companies have to be better at absorbing misfits now. There are a lot more misfits in the younger generation. Everyone is more of an individual now. People are freer to be their unique selves." Whether or not traditional companies can accommodate a growing misfit population remains to be seen.

Today Berdish is retired, but his misfit streak holds strong. "When I was a little boy, the first thing I wanted to be when I grew up was a pirate. Now I live by the James River and am working on sustainable shipping projects on the Great Lakes, the northeast U.S. coast, and Virginia." Berdish credits his work ethic and his ability to be both optimistic and passionate about change as key drivers throughout his career.

AT A TIME WHEN THE FINANCIAL SYSTEM IS IN NEED OF RADICAL REFORM, housing markets are facing ongoing disruption, and the energy sector is facing severe long-term challenges; when local communities are facing crises ranging from unemployment to water scarcity, spiraling mental health issues to reported decreases in human happiness and well-being, we must all ask ourselves: How can we best harness the instinct to innovate? How can we help companies develop businesses that are socially and environmentally responsible, that can recruit and retain the next generation of talent and serve the needs of society?

Now is the time to look elsewhere for novel ways of rebuilding and reshaping what commitment to old thought has destroyed.

Now is the time to look to misfits.

FIVE WAYS OF UNLEASHING YOUR INNER MISFIT

Following our journey through the world of misfits, we have distilled five key principles for unleashing your inner misfit: Hustle, Copy, Hack, Provoke, and Pivot. Each of these principles is covered in depth in its own chapter in Part Two.

Our ambition is to show what we can learn from the fringe and how to adapt that learning for our own purposes. The reality is that most of us will never join the criminal underground in Mexico or live in the urban slums of India, and that is a good thing. But we all have an "inner misfit"—parts of ourselves that do not conform to conventional norms or that hold viewpoints that do not align with the majority.

Our goal is to empower you to apply the insights you gather about yourself and from the cases in this book to your own industry, company, career, or community. We hope you will be inspired by the frugality, determination, and scrappiness of the underground, as well as motivated to channel your own energies into hacking our private- and public-sector systems so that they live up to our ideals.

Part 2

UNLEASHING YOUR INNER MISFIT

Chapter 2

HUSTLE

GROWING UP, FABIAN RUIZ KNEW HE WANTED TO DO SOMETHING THAT RE-
quired a suit and tie. Hard work, his parents always told him,
is something to be admired. *"Para adelante siempre, y nunca para
atrás, ni para coger impulso."* Keep moving forward, never go
backward, not even to catch a boost.

In 1972 his family—mom, dad, and then-four-year-old
brother, Carlos—moved from Colombia to New Jersey, where
Fabian was born the next year. Before Ruiz turned one, his
family moved a last time: to Jamaica, Queens, in New York.
There he would develop into a quiet, studious, structure-
loving kid. When he finished fourth grade, Fabian's parents
decided to move him to a private school, after witnessing his
older brother's involvement in gang violence at the local public

school. His favorite subject at his private Catholic prep school, St. John's, was science. "I loved new ideas," he recalled.

His parents and his brother were his heroes. He looked up to his father, a trained accountant who worked at a chemical fluid factory, later moving on to employment in several large banks. He admired his mother, a secretary, for her ability to juggle housework and a full-time job. And his brother? "My brother was my everything," said Ruiz, dressed in a sharp suit, his tie centered perfectly.

That is where Ruiz's story starts.

THE RUIZ FAMILY'S NEIGHBORS KNEW THE BROTHERS WERE CLOSE, THAT Carlos would always come to Fabian's aid if needed. "And that is why," he told us, his voice breaking, "I was known to never be scared of anything; if something ever went wrong, my brother would be there to fix it."

Fabian and his brother were playing baseball in a park in Jamaica, Queens, when their lives changed forever. Carlos, along with some of his friends, left the game early, while Fabian and the rest of the crew stayed to play out the innings. When Fabian stopped by a friend's house after the game to return a borrowed glove, his friend told him where his brother had gone. The night before, Carlos had been shot at outside a grocery store, and friends had arranged for him to meet with his aggressor a few blocks away. "I made up my mind right there," Fabian said. "Someone was going to get killed, and it wasn't going to be my brother." He quickly made his way to the intersection where his brother was waiting with two friends. Carlos told him, "Get out of here. You're not supposed to be here." Fabian said, "I'm not leaving," and as they proceeded to argue, Carlos's adversary drove up in a white sedan.

At sixteen years of age, Fabian Ruiz shot and killed his brother's adversary. It was his first and last violent crime. He would be tried for second-degree murder and sent to New York City's Rikers Island.

IN THE EARLY DAYS OF HIS INCARCERATION, RUIZ BEGAN TO THINK LIKE A prisoner. The sheer desperation of his situation forced him to develop the hustler's instinct: a determination to take his destiny into his own hands; an ingenuity that would allow him to make something out of nothing.

Illustrating this resourcefulness, Ruiz rose from his chair during our interview. He stood tall, broad-shouldered, commanding. "Look around this room," he said. "There are at least a hundred weapons in here." We looked at him, perplexed. "You see that piece of plastic on that chair? I could melt that and turn it into a razor." He pointed to a metal rod on a TV stand and said he could fashion it into a sword. The entire plumbing system in the building, he said, was an arsenal of weapons. "That speaker in the corner? I could take it apart and find something, anything, in there that could be transformed into a weapon."

Fabian's instinctive urge to hustle—to create his own op-portunities rather than sitting back passively to watch his fate unfold—led him to attempt an escape. On Rikers Island, the prisoners were grouped by different classifications. There were cells, and there were "mods," or small trailers. "They stuck me in a mod . . . and I realized . . . these things are made out of Sheetrock and tin. I'm facing twenty-five years to life, and you're gonna stick me in Sheetrock and tin?"

Fabian observed and analyzed every detail of his surround-ings. Every wall, every crevice, every corner. Eventually, he noticed an exhaust system, with birds flying in and out. He wondered, "How did they get in there?" If there's a way in, he told us, there must be a way out. "That's it. I followed the birds."

One night, two friends distracted the corrections officer on duty long enough for Fabian to unlock the door to the slop sink (the large sink in the mop closet open only to the "house gang" who cleaned the mods) and slip out through the ceiling. A friend slept in his bed during the routine overnight check in order to buy time and delay suspicion. At two A.M., Fabian emerged on the roof of the mod. The ground was a long way down. He jumped from roof to roof across a seemingly endless stream of trailers, looking out over the fences to the parking lot and the water beyond.

His original plan to sneak out through the parking lot was not an option: Corrections officers were smoking and talk-ing around the entrance. He changed directions and found an empty escape route, jumping to the ground and over the first two fences separating him from freedom. The last fence stood about twenty feet tall and was covered in barbed wire in all directions. Fabian could smell the salt water on the other side. He threw a blanket over the barbed wire and tried to ignore the pain and climb. It was impossible. The fence was embedded in concrete, eliminating the option of a tunnel. As sunlight began to lighten the sky, he felt queasy. He hid under a construction trailer, hoping to remain there until nightfall, when he would try again. At seven A.M., an alarm went off through the facility. Helicopters circled overhead, and the feet of corrections officers swarmed around him. Eventually, dogs were released to sniff him out, and he heard a corrections officer say into her walkie-talkie: "I think I got him."

"I could see the water," he told us.

FABIAN WAS SENTENCED TO AN ADDITIONAL YEAR FOR HIS ATTEMPTED EScape, and his classification was deemed "CMC Max A" (centrally monitored case, maximum security). He spent the next several months in the "bing" (solitary confinement), where he realized that his hustle could be applied in more positive ways.

Slowly, he reverted to his quiet and studious self. He spent his time reading everything from comic books to the classics, *Time* magazine to the Bible, the Torah, and the Koran. Deemed a threat to order since his attempted escape, he was moved constantly from one cell to another and between prisons. He avoided joining a prison gang, which in the early nineties was an exception to the norm.

He began to study New York criminal law, gaining a paralegal certificate, spending hours roving through law books and past cases, writing motions, and filing reports. He worked as a law clerk, which was one of the most significant experiences in his life. "Finally, in that information, I saw the key to a long-locked door." He told us that many people who spend time in prison do so out of their inability to use information in a way that translates to mainstream society. A true hustler, he realized that you have to use what is at your disposal wisely.

It wasn't only knowledge of the law that Ruiz pursued. He also acquired an associate's degree in liberal arts from a community college. He got certified as a plumber's helper, an electrician's helper, in asbestos removal, in HIV prevention, in youth assistance, in anti-violence. He started *The Rap Tablet*, a hip-hop and prison newsmagazine.

He navigated these disparate worlds during the twenty-one years he served in prison. "I learned everything about life in prison. I spent my eighteenth, my twenty-first, my everything, in that big house." All the while he was learning, observing, honing the skills that he could utilize upon his release at thirty-eight. He wrote down his business ideas in a notebook. "I left it in prison on the day I left, but I'll never forget it. It's in my head, nobody can ever take it from me, and it informs—always—everything I do now."

When Ruiz stepped outside on the day of his release, "I felt wobbly," he recalled. "The floor just didn't feel right." But he had a new set of skills that he was taking with him into the world.

ON THE DAY WE INTERVIEWED RUIZ, HE HAD BEEN OUT OF PRISON FOR EX-
actly 360 days. The hustle, which Ruiz had honed during his
incarceration, is now being applied in positive ways in the outside world. At the time of writing, he is participating in Defy
Ventures, a New York City–based nonprofit program designed
to help ex-offenders start their own businesses. In a major
mainstream nod to what some might see as a fringe enterprise,
Defy is privately funded by executives and foundations to "provide carefully selected, ambitious men and women who have
criminal histories with life-changing entrepreneurship, leadership, and career opportunities."

Ruiz's business is Infor-Nation, a start-up that serves as a
mail-order research tool dedicated to connecting prisoners to
online legal information and search engine queries. For many
reasons, the Internet is not available to most prisoners. When
Ruiz was in prison, his family sent him printed information
from the Web to assist in his case and in figuring out what to
do when he got home. With the aid of the Internet and his
mastery of the library, he helped others with appeals, motion
writing, and report filing.

Ruiz had an idea: What if I could offer a service to other
prisoners? Be that person who brings the outside world to the
inside? And since all mail leaving and entering prison gets read,
why would it be a problem if an inmate requests a printed message from Facebook, an email, or information that would be
helpful to him when his sentence is served?

Following his earlier victory in Defy's "Cinco de Mayo" competition, which provided him two thousand dollars of initial grant funding for Infor-Nation, he was accepted into an incubator program where he further developed his business plan. Like a true hustler, Ruiz is toiling as a construction worker to pay the bills—"the only job I could find, with my record," he told us—while working hard to grow Infor-Nation.

"When you invest in this business," Ruiz urged the judges, "you're investing not just in me, but in people whose total and complete isolation from our world—this world—harms society greatly."

Ruiz (and virtually every other former offender we spoke with) referred to the importance of passion in keeping the hustle going. "I've always been all in," he told us. When he was a kid, he jumped off a building while wearing a makeshift cape. "I was so sure I could fly," he said, laughing. In prison, you live with a similar all-or-nothing mentality. If you're going to get in a fight, you'd better fight with all you have or you'll die. "You can't just throw a punch and leave," Ruiz offered.

As our conversation with Ruiz came to a close, he noticed a line written on one of our notebooks: "What do pirates, terrorists, computer hackers, and inner-city gangs have in common with Silicon Valley? Innovation." Ruiz commented: "That's interesting. What's the difference between us and some guys from Silicon Valley? Other than better decision making as young kids, nothing."

Our last question to Ruiz? His thoughts on capitalism. "What's good about capitalism?" he asked. "The hustle. I respect the hustle. I respect the liberty to find opportunity in anything and to act on it."

THE HUSTLE

"Contrary to popular opinion," the author and comedian Fran Lebowitz once quipped, "the hustle is not a new dance step—it is an old business procedure." Old it may be, but today "hustle" is an oft-heard word in the business world. Employment ads, particularly for small businesses, sometimes cite hustle as a requirement for aspiring applicants.

Historically, the word "hustle" was used to describe obtaining something illicitly or through forceful action, or undertaking a fraud, a con, or a swindle. The modern usage is changing, however, and modern management lingo is now replete with references to the hustle, hustling, and hustlers.

In the lexicon of the Misfit Economy, we define "hustle" as making something out of nothing. To move fast, to trade one thing for another, and to proactively create your own opportunities rather than waiting for opportunity to come your way. To hustle means getting your hands dirty, being lean and facile, working hard, being resourceful and resilient, and showing or having gumption, chutzpah, or mojo.

Hustle is about getting things done, just like Fabian Ruiz did during his period of incarceration. It's about being resourceful, opportunity-driven, and frugal—learning to do a lot with a little, to create your own destiny. A flexible mind-set allows you to move seamlessly from one world to another, borrowing from one and bringing new perspective to the next. An effective hustler does this seamlessly, transposing conceptual frameworks, making useful and valuable connections, and bringing skills and competencies from one area to another.

When you are hustling, there is no master plan; you are improvising and being responsive to what life throws your way. The hustle is about spotting an idea and just going for it. You don't need massive resources, a perfect team, or the right environment. Much of innovation comes from constraint—from challenge and even scarcity.

FROM PRIVATE EQUITY TO PRISON CELLS

Defy Ventures, the program helping Fabian Ruiz establish Infor-Nation, was founded by Catherine (Cat) Hoke.

Hoke had auspicious beginnings as a venture capitalist in Palo Alto and New York City, as well as a fledgling career in private equity. At age twenty-five, she went to Romania to volunteer with HIV-infected kids in an orphanage. Upon her return, Hoke told us, she started "praying for an opportunity to combine my new heart for injustice with my passion for business."

Hoke was dissatisfied with private equity. She craved a more meaningful life of love and service. In her words, "Dying with a big pile of money didn't appeal to me."

When she was twenty-six, her prayers were answered after she embarked upon a church mission that took her to a prison in Texas, a trip that would change the course of her life. During this visit, instead of seeing the prisoners as guilty, she saw them as potential entrepreneurs, many of whom possessed the characteristics she sought in the start-ups presented to her as a venture capitalist.

That same year, Hoke and her husband moved to Texas, where she founded Prison Entrepreneurship Program (PEP). Hoke invested her entire savings in the program, and by 2008 it was already operating with a budget of $3.2 million, about sixty times her initial investment.

In the ten years since, PEP has been hailed as a tremendous success in preparing prisoners for reentry into civilian life, via classes on topics from how to start a new business to how to bridge the past with a more positive, productive future.

PEP's 2011–2012 annual report states that the program has a 5 percent recidivism rate (much lower than the U.S. average of 40 percent), meaning that only 5 percent of former offenders have gone on to "reoffend." (One gathers that they were meaningfully redirecting their energies into more productive, profitable, and legal endeavors, thanks to PEP.) In five years, five hundred students graduated from PEP; around sixty started their own businesses. Many of them have become employers themselves. By imagining and implementing PEP, Hoke pivoted from the world of private equity to work with prison populations. But her story doesn't end there.

Hoke left Texas in 2009, after admitting to inappropriate relationships with four of PEP's graduates. The Texas Department of Criminal Justice had threatened to close the program as long as Hoke was involved. She resigned. She went from being something of a hero for a worthy cause to someone in the crosshairs of a scandal. "I didn't want to live anymore," Hoke told us. She was certain this was her downfall.

But Hoke picked herself up and hustled, just as she had been teaching PEP's ex-prisoners to do. Hustling is having the tenacity to pick yourself up in the face of repeated failure, and reaching down deep to rally the energy and passion required to make something happen. It means to keep moving, not giving up, changing direction based on constant feedback and learning. To hustle is to force destiny, to create serendipity by outweighing or outwitting negativity with positive energy.

Hoke invoked this spirit and moved to New York City, where she founded Defy Ventures. As part of the course, a year-long MBA-style program, ex-cons spend up to sixteen hours a week learning business basics: how to come up with a name for a company, the dos and don'ts of intellectual property, how to speak in public, how to read a balance sheet. The students write business plans and compete for seed money to fund their ventures.

Since 2010, Defy Ventures has generated over $13 million in income for ex-offenders, or "entrepreneurs-in-training" (EITs). At the time of writing, 115 EITs have graduated from the program; they've launched 72 companies, all incubated and funded by Defy. These companies have created 35 new employment opportunities. The program has an 87 percent employment rate and recidivism of under 5 percent, and grads have reported an income increase of 94 percent within six months of participating with Defy.

We spoke with other participants in the Defy program, and we found that many of them shared Fabian Ruiz's finely honed hustling ability, seeing opportunity in everything. "I don't care what it is," one Defy entrepreneur told us, "I can make money out of it."

Another Defy alumnus, Luis Martinez, a former drug dealer who started Brooklyn Joe Painters, a painting and remodeling company, said that the ways he changed his life were informed by what he learned in order to survive in prison: to use what he had and not lose energy focusing on what he didn't; to utilize the work ethic he learned on the streets; to do what it took to get the job done.

Jose Vasquez is a former drug dealer who made over $750,000 selling heroin. Nobody makes that kind of money standing on a street corner waiting for the occasional passerby. Vasquez built distribution channels. He developed a unique brand and packaging, implemented quality control, managed a team, and offered dependable customer service. From his life as a dealer, he learned hustling skills that are applicable to the formal economy, and today, through Defy Ventures, Vasquez is teaching other former drug dealers and ex-cons how to parlay their particular street skills into legal activities, so they may find jobs in mainstream industries or start their own businesses.

The Defy curriculum blends traditional business training, such as how to write a résumé and a business plan, with more soft-skill training around communication and personal development. The Defy program also builds fun into its training.

As Hoke told us, "For a lot of these guys who have come from the streets and been in prison, they've always faced enormous pressure. A lot of them never really got a childhood." Part of the program aims to connect the Defy participants with humor and lightness so they can recapture some of that lost innocence. Defy Ventures is one of a number of programs worldwide that aim to capture this spirit.

Baillie Aaron, a Harvard graduate, founded Venturing Out, a prison entrepreneurship program based in Boston. When we asked why she started the program, she told us of her time as a GED tutor in a prison, during which she helped people in prison study for the exam, in one case being asked to take a student from a third-grade to a twelfth-grade equivalency education. One of her students changed the way Aaron viewed people in prison. "When you explained a math problem in the traditional way—using apples or pies or pencils—he struggled to understand how to solve it. But when I used sales or profit as examples for math problems, he understood the solution instantly. Many people in the criminal justice system have an advanced understanding of business, sales, and profit."

Aaron offered some insight into why people who have committed crimes can make outstanding legal entrepreneurs. Because they often grow up in challenging circumstances, she told us, people in prison tend to be more resilient and thus able to better deal with challenges that come from running a business of your own. And because of their difficult backgrounds, Aaron said, many of her students were exceptionally observant and alert to their surroundings, which, in her experience, enhanced their ability to read people and to spot trends and patterns.

Research supports the idea that some of those who have been to prison for committing a crime do possess entrepreneurial aptitude. Matthew C. Sonfield of Hofstra University conducted research[1] that found prison inmates had a high ability for entrepreneurship. Another study, "Does Entrepreneurship Pay? The Michael Bloombergs, the Hot Dog Vendors, and the Returns to Self-Employment," by Ross Levine and Yona Rubinstein, tried to determine what makes a successful entrepreneur. In the study, Levine and Rubinstein define an entrepreneur as someone who engages in inventive or risky activity (like Bill Gates or Michael Bloomberg), rather than a self-employed entrepreneur (like a plumber or a carpenter). Amid the characteristics that make a successful entrepreneur, one stood out: juvenile delinquency. The authors found that those who had been involved in "aggressive, illicit and risky activities" in their teen years were more likely to go on to be successful entrepreneurs.[2]

Today there are 2.4 million people locked up in the United States.[3] It is a near-impossible task for ex-offenders to find worthwhile and meaningful employment after their release, as most places of business are reluctant to hire people with criminal records. Ex-offenders who remain unemployed have a three to five times higher chance of committing another crime than those who find employment.[4] The entrepreneurship schooling and guidance provided by people like Cat Hoke and Baillie Aaron is a way to help solve the challenge of reintegrating ex-offenders into society, while at the same time transferring skills acquired from a life of crime into a life in the formal economy. Hoke calls it "transforming the hustle."

LIKE FABIAN RUIZ, MANY OF THE EX-PRISONERS IN PROGRAMS SUCH AS DEFY Ventures and Venturing Out have cultivated a mind-set of re-sourcefulness and frugality that is at the core of the hustling spirit: a willingness to use everything at one's disposal to help achieve goals. Effective hustlers focus on what they have, not what they lack, and find novel ways to use all of the tools they have access to. They also know that you don't have to wait for every element to be perfect before launching a venture; they start from a garage or a bedroom, like Apple and Virgin Records did, even if all the ingredients aren't in place.

Hustling is not for the faint of heart or spirit. It may take weeks, months, even years for efforts to bear fruit, meaning that stamina and endurance are essential weapons in the hustler's arsenal.

FORMER PRISONERS AND REFORMED CRIMINALS ARE NOT THE ONLY PEOPLE who are hustling. We live in a time when financial crisis has gripped many of the world's economies for over half a decade, making it harder than ever for the "less established" (individuals and businesses alike) to carve out a niche and prosper.

In Spain, where recession has deepened in the years following the global financial crisis of 2008–2009, and where the youth unemployment rate is close to 50 percent, many are hustling in the informal economy for subsistence. "Without the underground economy," Robert Tornabell, a professor and former dean of the ESADE Business School in Barcelona, told the *New York Times*, "we would be in a situation of probably violent social unrest. . . . A lot of people are now staying afloat only thanks to the underground economy, as well as the support of their family network."[5]

Spaniards are doing what it takes to get by in difficult times. Flea markets and retail stores that run on the principle of barter are emerging across the country. Whereas in the past, secondhand goods carried a stigma for Spaniards, they have become a common response to the economic crisis. At the same time, Internet-based platforms—so-called time banks— have allowed Spaniards to exchange services, skills, knowledge, and trades. These platforms permit unemployed and underemployed individuals to exchange what they do have for goods and services that they need.

This trend toward "collaborative consumption" is taking place worldwide. As Rachel Botsman and Roo Rogers chronicle in their book, *What's Mine Is Yours*, sharing, trading, and selling idle items, time, and services is a rising trend. From Airbnb (a rental website that has gone from 120,000 listings in early 2012 to over 300,000 at the time of this writing) to Zipcar (the car-sharing service that was sold to Avis for $500 million in January 2013), people the world over are moving away from the fixed, formal "own it" model to a more fluid "exchange it" approach.

The importance of the informal economy is starting to become more apparent in other European countries. In the United Kingdom, a September 2012 study[6] by the Royal Society of Arts (RSA) and Community Links found that the informal economy was flourishing, and that its existence was, in fact, *important* to the health of entrepreneurship. A nod to the need for hustle, this study underscored that in order for entrepreneurs to formalize their activities (as in, legally become a taxpaying registered business), they often have to trade one skill for another—exchange a website design for a marketing strategy, for example, or pay a supplier off the books. And because registering a business comes with many regulatory hurdles—heavy taxes, little financial credit, hours of cutting through red tape—the YouGov poll taken for the report found that 20 percent of small-business owners had "traded informally" (hustled) during the early days of their company.

A common misperception is that those who work informally are trying to cheat the government of taxes in order to take more money home. Some do. In the UK, as much as £200 billion (about $328 billion) arises from and is spent on undeclared work per year.[7] However, informality is an important step in nurturing the rise of small business.

In an economy ravaged by crisis, it seems prudent to encourage entrepreneurship by any means possible. Forty percent of the one in five small-business owners surveyed by the RSA said that, when setting up, they had engaged in hustling, or informal trading, because it gave them "the breathing space before they had the capacity to register their business." Only 9 percent said they did it to bring in additional income.

Moreover, in the United States, the spirit of hustling is mainstreaming because of the growth of the freelance economy. It's estimated that by 2020, 40 percent of the American workforce will be freelance, contract, and temporary workers.[8] Without traditional jobs, many are seeking diverse and creative sources of income and are working to take advantage of entrepreneurial opportunities.

IT TAKES A CRISIS

In 2008, an economic crisis hit Wilmington, Ohio. The international shipping company DHL cut around nine thousand jobs in Wilmington and the surrounding Clinton County. The county went from having one of the lowest unemployment rates in Ohio to having the highest. At that time, twenty-five-year-old Mark Rembert had just received his acceptance into the Peace Corps and was waiting to go to Ecuador. After serving nine months, Taylor Stuckert, his childhood friend, had been evacuated from his Peace Corps placement in Bolivia due to political instability.

Shortly after the announcement of the job losses at DHL, Lehman Brothers collapsed and the global financial crisis hit. "The economy seemed to be crumbling around us," Rembert said. Rather than pursuing international development via the Peace Corps, he and Stuckert recognized the crisis in their own community and decided to spend the year making a difference locally.

It was a mental adjustment. As Stuckert said, "I stopped looking for the next move and just told myself, 'I'm here, I have to try to work to change things.'" The two friends shifted from being consumers of a place to producers. "When you are local, you can't complain. If you think the culture or politics or entertainment of a town sucks, you have to do something about it," Stuckert told us. One of the first campaigns they spearheaded was "buy local," in which they created awareness around local businesses and encouraged citizens to purchase from these companies. The campaign engaged 250 participating businesses and activated over 4,000 consumers. During the course of the campaign, local purchasing increased by over 25 percent.

Often we think of hustle as being connected with stories of cowboy-style "Lone Ranger" entrepreneurship, built around the extraordinary efforts and endurance of one individual. But Rembert and Stuckert were hoping to catalyze community hustle; they didn't want the community to sit passively and wait for economic recovery. "For us, it was about not depending on corporations or politicians and external investment anymore," Stuckert told us.

They've triggered a number of local interventions under the banner of their nonprofit, Energize Clinton County. Building on their experiences with the Peace Corps model of economic development, they established a community fellows program, which connects local youth with small businesses that need support. They've continued to expand the influence of their buy-local campaign, which is now being scaled across six county regions in south central Ohio. Rembert and Stuckert have also worked with the city to install commercial solar panels and are working with private- and public-sector partners to generate more investment in local alternative energy. The list of projects goes on—from catalyzing farmers' markets to building professional and coding skills as a means of preventing brain drain from the city.

One of their most impressive feats was taking over the chamber of commerce, which had been plagued with debt and poor management. "We wanted the chamber to really be a platform and source of support for local businesses," they told us. Since then, they have recruited more than a hundred new members and created a new website and a weekly newsletter to keep members informed about opportunities.

While there is no longer an economic crisis, the two friends' challenge now is keeping the community motivated to remain economically resilient without big business. "DHL was a consequence of short-term thinking," Stuckert told us. "The company received over half a billion dollars in public funds for jobs that lasted for only around five years. But DHL wasn't the problem. It was a wake-up call." The irony is that if DHL asked to come back tomorrow, Rembert and Stuckert think the county would open their arms. "But we shouldn't be spending our public dollars and giving it away to international corporations," they said. "We need to invest locally and in small businesses." Rembert and Stuckert are focused on keeping the drumbeat of community hustle alive, making sure the town doesn't slip back into dependency on big business.

Their advice to others to kick-start community hustle? "You have to learn to be a catalyst and not a dictator. Having a charismatic personality certainly helps move things, but it's less about one person. The biggest thing is learning how to get out of the way of things," Stuckert told us. A lot of their process for engaging community has been about really asking people in town what they want Wilmington to become in the future. "Getting a community to be self-critical, where people feel like they are shaping the economic priorities, is key," Rembert said.

Many define hustle as leaving behind a small town in pursuit of success in a bigger city, but Rembert and Stuckert offer a different script. They invested locally, applying their international development expertise to their hometown. For both Rembert and Stuckert, staying put in Wilmington was not only about the opportunity to make a difference; it also forced them to confront things about themselves and grow personally. "Rather than running away from things, you have to unpack your feelings of discomfort about a place. And most of those problems you have about a place are really problems you have with yourself," Rembert told us. It's a refreshing perspective. In an age of hyper-mobility and migration, when every opportunity can instill a fear of missing out, small-town life seems to offer an antidote.

Rembert and Stuckert aren't alone. Across the United States and particularly in the Southeast and the Rust Belt, misfits are bringing a do-it-yourself spirit to revitalize communities and boost economic recovery. Greensboro, Alabama, is another town facing economic hardship but hoping to rebound thanks to the hustle of its community.

Historically a prosperous part of the cotton economy, Greensboro is struggling. Catfish is a big part of the economy today, but the area is largely poor, with little local industry. In Hale County, we spoke to Pam Dorr, a misfit working to develop community hustle. Originally from California, Dorr worked with big brands like Victoria's Secret, Esprit, and babyGap before moving to rural Alabama ten years ago. Initially, she came as a volunteer to build low-cost affordable housing in Hale County, but she fell in love with the place and never left.

In 1994, after she finished volunteering, she started a project called HERO, focused on catalyzing community development and ending rural poverty in the Alabama Black Belt. The median income in Hale County is $22,000 a year.[9]

Dorr is working through HERO with committed citizens to create economic opportunities. The economic experiments initiated by HERO include a local thrift store, a day-care center, a bike manufacturing shop, a pie shop, a jewelry production line, and even a pajama line (which is launching soon). She also works with high school dropouts, offering youth education and connecting these young people to training programs with some of her businesses. "I didn't have a master plan," she told us. "You can't be afraid to make a mistake. It's trial and error."

Dorr tells us that the Greensboro area has had a lot of outbound migration. Her work has focused on building skills and jump-starting the local economy so that people can feel proud to walk down Main Street. "In a small town, the work I do counts," Dorr said. "You can see and feel the impact."

Communities igniting rural hustle in places like Greensboro, Alabama, and Wilmington, Ohio, are fostering greater local economic resilience and self-sufficiency, inspiring communities to take back their economic agency.

ON THE FIRST PAGES OF THIS BOOK, WE INTRODUCED WALID ABDUL-WAHAB, the young man seeking to build up the camel milk trade in the United States through his company Desert Farms.

The small population of camels in the United States presents a significant hurdle for those seeking to grow the country's camel milk industry. Part of the challenge lies in the fact that increasing the number of female camels to meet a growing demand for camel milk will necessarily result in a comparable increase in the number of male camels. There is no immediately apparent commercial use for males, given the very limited demand for camel meat in the United States, which presents a challenge for putative camel farmers. Import restrictions also represent a significant barrier.

The history of camels in the United States dates back to the mid-1850s, as relayed to us by Doug Baum, a Texas-born U.S. camel historian. Baum was formerly a zookeeper in Nashville, Tennessee, who gave camel rides to children. While he found limited pleasure in his job, he tells us that he "really dug the camels." Visitors to the zoo would often give him books about the animals. One day he received one that detailed the history of camels in the United States. He devoured the book, quit his job, and bought two camels. Baum now travels the world, telling the story.

Camels were first brought to the United States by government officials as an alternative mode of transport for the army in the arid Southwest. By 1855, Congress had approved thirty-thousand dollars for the purchase of camels. The cause was taken up by none other than Confederate leader Jefferson Davis, who helped rally support for the "U.S. Camel Corps."

Following the Civil War, the camels were sold into private hands. Since that time, camels have remained largely outside the mainstream of American society. At the time of writing, according to Baum, "a little over two thousand Arabian camels and three to five hundred Bactrian camels reside in the United States. Many are zoo or circus stock, but most are privately held by perhaps as many as twenty or thirty individuals who breed, sell, or work camels. Herd numbers range between eight and eighty camels, and significant numbers dwell piecemeal around the country on private game ranches."

Despite the challenges, Abdul-Wahab and his suppliers have persisted, and their efforts are yielding promising initial results, albeit on a small scale. They do have one thing in their favor: a slowly growing pool of demand, as word slowly but surely spreads about the medicinal qualities of the mythical "white gold" harvested from the camels.

While Abdul-Wahab is careful to not make any claims

about the health benefits of camel milk, he does acknowledge that 90 percent of his customers are the parents of autistic children.

THE CAMEL MILK INDUSTRY IS A QUINTESSENTIAL MISFIT ECONOMY. THE MILK is derived from a strange animal—not particularly beautiful or charismatic, never accepted by the mainstream (at least not in the United States), a true misfit of the animal world. The product is also unusual, a drink with mythical health benefits that are widely believed but not scientifically proven. The trade is everything but straightforward—the camel milk protagonists we spoke with all described navigating the economy as a real challenge, with patchwork regulation, at least in the United States, and a barrage of bureaucratic hurdles. Yet there exists a highly committed group of people determined to drive the industry forward.

In his experiences within this particular Misfit Economy, Walid Abdul-Wahab represents the true spirit of hustling. For Abdul-Wahab, getting Desert Farms off the ground has not been easy: managing his parents' expectations, overcoming legislative hurdles and battling the FDA, countering cultural resistance to his product, formalizing business relationships with technologically resistant Amish farmers, and battling to grow his industry despite the small camel population. With drive and determination, Abdul-Wahab relentlessly pursues his goal of building a large-scale, commercially successful camel milk business.

Hustle is about spotting an idea and going for it, and that is exactly what Abdul-Wahab did in a journey that began with a Ziploc bag of camel milk and ended with the creation of a business that has the potential to establish a new industry in the United States.

FROM THE EX-PRISONERS WE INTERVIEWED, TO THE RURAL HUSTLERS WE met rebuilding small towns, to the camel milk protagonists we encountered, we saw proof of the tenacity and resourcefulness that exists throughout the Misfit Economy. A hustler doesn't wait for the perfect conditions to unfold. A true hustler takes destiny into his own hands, using whatever tools he has at his disposal, propelling himself forward with an irrepressible will to succeed and determination to survive.

Chapter 3

COPY

WATER MARGIN, KNOWN IN CHINESE AS *SHUIHU ZHUAN,* IS A FOURTEENTH-century novel that depicts the life of Song Jiang, an outlaw who helps the poor by stealing from the rich. It is a story that many have likened to that of Robin Hood and his merry men. And now, it seems, this narrative has found fresh application in the copycat culture of Chinese innovation.

Throughout China, entrepreneurs are "robbing the rich" of intellectual property through a process known as *shanzhai.* The term refers to pirated or imitation brands and goods. But the concept encompasses more than knockoff products. It is also about adapting products to consumer tastes. While some argue that shanzhai is outright theft, others point to its ingenuity in not only imitating existing products but also enhancing and adapting technologies for local markets and lower-income consumers.

Many innovators in China and India argue that appropriating the intellectual property of larger, predominantly Western companies is an ethical duty, particularly when these companies fail to price their products affordably. Shanzhai is a modern-day solution for a historical Robin Hood dilemma: In the face of tyrannical rule, rob the rich to supply the poor.

This appropriation is acute across fast-moving consumer good technologies. The best-documented instances of shanzhai are in the telecom industry, where shanzhai innovators sell mobile phones for as little as a fifth of the price of name brands. Beyond mobile, the "shanzhai sector" is expanding into more sophisticated product lines. Shanzhai electric cars are being built and sold for as little as two to three thousand dollars in Shandong Province. By contrast, new electric cars such as the Nissan Leaf, Chevy Volt, and Toyota Prius cost upward of twenty thousand. Many shanzhai innovators cater to China's mass market better than foreign multinationals, given the domestic advantage of knowing the customer base and its price points.

Consider BYD, a local business that started out by producing and selling knockoff Toyota cars at half the price. Founded in 1995 with family money and beginning with only twenty employees (it now has more than ten thousand), BYD has moved beyond its shanzhai roots to become one of China's most successful legitimate automobile manufacturers. In 2013, BYD became the tenth largest automobile brand, selling more than half a million passenger cars in China.[1] Its owner, Wang Chuanfu, is now among the world's five hundred richest people, according to *Forbes*.

Within the Misfit Economy, the copying strategies employed by shanzhai innovation are smart and lucrative. Copying provides a running start for small local businesses and start-ups because they are able to leverage a market that has already been established and proved by the original product. This creates a quick, reliable revenue stream. In other instances, such as BYD, shanzhai serves as a temporary strategy, providing a means of catching up with incumbent companies and transferring manufacturing skills. After gaining traction, companies may then choose to distance themselves from their shanzhai roots, as they mature and seek to protect their newly built market share.

Ultimately, this Robin Hood approach to IP is nothing new. The United States went through its own shanzhai period during its industrial development, when it ripped off patents from Europe. In the late eighteenth and early nineteenth centuries, the mechanical designs of cotton mills and spinning machines were taken from England and smuggled into the United States by skilled machinists.[2] As Doron S. Ben-Atar writes in *Trade Secrets*, "Lax enforcement of the intellectual property laws was the primary engine of the American economic miracle."

Ultimately, shanzhai is not about creating unique new products. It's about mashing up different elements that are in the formal marketplace completely separate. For example, you and I can buy either an iPhone or an Android, or you can buy either a MacBook or a Windows-run PC. End of story. Shanzhai innovators look to what isn't on the menu: a smartphone that looks like an iPhone but runs on Android, or a laptop that looks like a Mac but runs Windows.

TO COPY OR NOT TO COPY

In the 1800s, the eccentric English writer Charles Caleb Colton said, "Imitation is the sincerest form of flattery." Flattering it may be, but copying is often the source of great anguish and aggravation for the party who has been imitated. Both culturally and legally (through the application of intellectual property law), there is a widely held view that ideas and creative output are proprietary. When this principle is breached through an act of copying, the person or group whose work has been misappropriated often feels that individuality, originality, and self-expression have been unfairly infringed upon and exploited.

Certainly, copying is not a new phenomenon. When Charles Dickens arrived in Boston in 1842, he was upset to find bookstores selling unauthorized copies of his work. Mark Twain filed a civil suit in Canada when he learned that cheap unauthorized editions of his books were being published and sold.

The market for counterfeit goods was once rampant within the food sector. As the *Boston Globe* reported:

A committee of would-be reformers who met in Boston in 1859 launched one of the first studies of American food purity, and their findings make for less-than-appetizing reading: candy was found to contain arsenic and dyed with copper chloride; conniving brewers mixed extracts of "nux vomica," a tree that yields strychnine, to simulate the bitter taste of hops. Pickles contained copper sulphate, and custard powders yielded traces of lead. Sugar was blended with plaster of Paris, as was flour. Milk had been watered down, then bulked up with chalk and sheep's brains. Hundred-pound bags of coffee labeled "Fine Old Java" turned out to consist of three-fifths dried peas, one-fifth chicory, and only one-fifth coffee.[3]

Today counterfeit products are growing seven times faster than legal goods; they make up about 10 percent of the world's trade. According to the International Anti-Counterfeiting Coalition, the international trade in pirated and fake goods amounts to $600 billion, comprising as much as 7 percent of global trade.[4]

In China, the home of shanzhai, pirating extends to retail stores, designs for buildings, even entire cities. In 2011 Chinese authorities in Kunming, southwest China, discovered twenty-two fake Apple stores. The employees donned the now-famous blue T-shirt and white lanyard; some perhaps believed they were working for Apple.[5] An office and retail complex in Beijing designed by the London architect Zaha Hadid was replicated in Chongqing, a major city in central China. In the Chinese province of Guangdong, you can find an exact replica of Hallstatt, a centuries-old Austrian village.[6]

— 81 —

Across every major city, there are blankets and tables of counterfeit goods lining the sidewalks: "designer" wallets and purses, watches, DVDs, and more. Nowhere is this phenomenon more evident than at the Chungking Mansions in Hong Kong, a mecca for copycat pirates. Described as "a ghetto at the center of the world" by anthropologist Gordon Matthews, Chungking Mansions is seventeen stories of gray- and black-market goods. Hawkers greet you at the door: "Louis Vuitton. Handbag, handbag." "Copy, copy, good price."

You can spend a day or stay the night in the hostels that line the upper floors of the building. Wandering around the mall-like interior during the day, you can purchase a masala curry from an Indian cook, share an elevator ride with a prostitute from Kenya, swap stories with a Nigerian pastor, and buy a knockoff phone from an Iranian electronics dealer.

Strolling amid the buyers and sellers are private investigators, often hired by multinational companies such as Microsoft and Pfizer to police the markets for copycat goods. Their job is to "bring to justice" the criminals responsible for selling counterfeit goods. However, the task of slowing down the shanzhai trade is seemingly impossible, given that the scale of counterfeiting in China has been enabled by lax government regulators who ignore many of the copycat markets. In Chungking Mansions, the building has security guards and an extensive CCTV surveillance system, but walking the premises, we were offered Class A drugs, fake DVDs, and imitation smartphones. The copycat trade here does not seem to be impeded by regulatory forces.

• • •

THE WORLD OF COPYCAT INNOVATION IS NOT LIMITED TO THE TYPES OF COUN-
terfeit consumer goods sold in Chungking Mansions. Since
the Internet revolution, with information so readily accessible,
products, services, even whole businesses can be cloned and
copied with ease.

The Berlin-based company Wimdu, for example, is an exact
replica of the successful platform Airbnb, a peer-to-peer rental
market that provides an alternative to hotels. Wimdu was built
by reverse-engineering Airbnb's functions and borrowing from
the site's look and feel. Illustrating the power of iteration over
pure invention, Wimdu created in a matter of months what
it had taken Airbnb four years to develop. By June 2011, the
company had raised over $90 million.[7]

Wimdu was started by three now-infamous German
brothers—Oliver, Marc, and Alexander Samwer—who have
a history of reverse-engineering U.S.-based innovations and
selling them back to the originator for a hefty price. They have
built companies that have been sold to eBay and Groupon and
have invested in German versions of U.S. innovations such as
YouTube, Twitter, and Facebook.

In a rare media appearance in *Wired*, Oliver Samwer explained the brothers' perspective: "We are builders of companies, we are not innovators. . . . Someone else is the architect
and we are the builders."[8]

Are there benefits to being a builder versus an innovator?
What are they? In his book *Copycats*, Oded Shenkar argues why

strategic imitators (or, as he calls them, "immovators") should be studied: "Imitators are less likely to become complacent, a significant problem for innovators and pioneers who are taken with their success to the point of underestimating the dangers lurking in the rearview mirror." Imitators, on the other hand, who "come from behind, tend to be paranoid about others following in their footsteps and are better prepared to repel the attack." Pioneers are often stuck in one way of doing things—the way they invented—while imitators are often more aware of transformational changes in the market precisely *because they imitated.*

As *Wired*'s Matt Cowan reported, in 1998 Marc Samwer had an instinct that eBay would thrive in the German market, as the country still suffered from old regulatory retail laws that prevented discounts (a vestige of its reunification in 1990, after the Berlin Wall crumbled). His brothers agreed. The Samwers told *Wired* that they contacted eBay via email numerous times, recommending that the company replicate the platform in Germany (and hire the Samwers to do so). Claiming that eBay failed to respond, the brothers started their own German-language auction site, Alando, which was then purchased by eBay for 38 million euros (over $50 million) only a hundred days after its debut. Had the Samwers not copied, eBay might have remained complacent, not realizing its potential within the German market.

Southwest Airlines, the low-cost U.S. giant, took one model (flying) and removed all the frills that most people didn't value, to offer a casual and inexpensive flying experience.

EasyJet and Ryanair (both European) then replicated South-west's idea, combining the fundamental model of low-cost flying with their own nuances. Ryanair went for the low-cost extreme, at one point proposing to charge for using the toilet, and offering "standing seats."[9]

As Shenkar writes in his book, Visa, MasterCard, and American Express copied Diners Club (the original credit card company), and the Japanese auto giant Toyota copied German engineering.

WHY COPY?

It is claimed by many that these copycats are immorally steal-ing the ideas of others, endangering our economy and jobs and even, in the case of some copycat products—such as counter-feit pharmaceuticals—risking lives. But is there anything that we can learn from them?

While we certainly do not advocate or condone the theft of intellectual property, we do believe that copying in the Misfit Economy can be beneficial and can play a role in helping to foster innovation.

Creativity in some industries thrives on copying, as Kal Raustiala and Christopher Sprigman found in their book, *The Knockoff Economy*. For example, the fashion industry remains innovative due to copying. Textile giants such as H&M, For-ever 21, and online shopping platform ASOS flourish by imi-tating designs originated by more expensive brands.

Defenders of copycats claim that such imitators are natural

competitors and are good for the economy. They help to break up monopolies and ensure innovation. Others argue that copying is a force for good in the world, bringing about incremental improvements and allowing products and functions to evolve. Intellectual property pirates, copycats, and those engaging in "collaborative innovation" can accelerate the diffusion of innovation and enable human progress. Henry Ford's assembly line, the personal computer, the Gutenberg press, the Internet: None of these innovations was a solitary in-a-vacuum, something-from-nothing, lightning-in-a-bottle creation. Innovating within the Misfit Economy often means building upon what has already been built, improving upon what exists already. All of these inventions were cumulative, collective; all happened step by step, idea upon idea, over time.

Many of us cleave to our own ideas. But part of learning to innovate is recognizing that other people sometimes have better ideas, and that what we think are "our" thoughts are not our ideas at all but ours to witness.

How often have you had what you were certain was an original thought or concept only to discover that others had it, too, either prior or simultaneously? The discovery of the double-helix structure of DNA is one example—James Watson and Francis Crick are known to have been working on the problem at the University of Cambridge while Rosalind Franklin and Maurice Wilkins at the University of London did the same.[10]

The theory of evolution, while largely accredited to Charles Darwin, was independently conceived by British biologist Alfred Russel Wallace. Wallace sent Darwin a letter outlining his theories of evolution. Darwin was shocked to find that Wallace's theories were almost identical to his own, which at the time were unpublished. The two went on to coauthor *On the Tendency of Species to Form Varieties, and on the Perpetuation of Varieties and Species by Natural Means of Selection*, the first publication about natural selection, in 1858. But it wasn't until Darwin published *On the Origins of Species* a year later that the public interest was really captured. *On the Origins of Species* was a compilation of research Darwin did nearly twenty years earlier, and the first printing of twenty-five hundred copies was already oversubscribed at the book's launch.

John Lienhard, author of *The Engines of Our Ingenuity* and retired professor of mechanical engineering and history at the University of Houston, describes this phenomenon best:

> Last year, two different men said to me, "I invented the heat pipe." Neither had ever heard of the other's work. And each really did invent the heat pipe. One described it in rudimentary form as early as 1937. The other created the modern form in 1962. Neither has profited from his invention. Each planted the seed. Each added to the collective unconscious of the technical community.[11]

This scenario invokes the notion of a collective unconscious or simultaneous invention. If an idea is "in the air" and capable of being thought of by many, can it be owned by anyone?

INVENTION IS COLLECTIVE

The term "collective invention" was popularized by economic historian Robert C. Allen in writing about one of the most mainstream, formal-market industries: steel. With steam engine technology, there were a plethora of firms eager to exchange information, practices, techniques, and designs, to the extent that no single inventor was responsible for major innovations in the steel sector. As Allen states with reference to the blast furnace industry in England:

> If one examines a sector like the blast furnace industry and determines the inventions whose diffusion were important for the growth in efficiency, it proves impossible to attribute their discovery to any single inventor. Certainly, no one received a patent for many of these advances. Thus, the increase in furnace height and blast temperature that were so important for productivity growth in England's Cleveland district evolved through the actions of many individuals over a twenty-year period.[12]

Historically, the open sharing of information was made necessary by high up-front investment costs associated with R&D, which couldn't be shouldered by an individual firm. As a result, R&D was not perceived as a competitive driver—it was a pre-competitive function, with many firms pooling resources. R&D was a misnomer altogether, for many firms didn't allocate resources to research and development (itself) but, rather, generated R&D or, more aptly, "technical material and know-how" as a by-product of normal investment. This information was then shared across firms to accelerate overall productivity.

While it seems contrary to share intellectual property, in the case of the steel industry, Allen writes, "collective invention spread costs among the firms in the industry."[13] Given the economic constraints of many small businesses in today's economy, this concept sounds far more prudent than far-fetched.

As relayed in Charlie Leadbeater's book, *We-Think*, the tin and copper mines in Cornwall, in the southwest of England, provide another example of how industries can succeed through the dissemination of intellectual property. To make the process of mining easier and safer, James Watt invented the now-well-known "Watt engine," a design that cut down the amount of coal required by two thirds.[14] Watt marketed and sold the engine with his partner, Matthew Boulton, spreading the innovation within the Cornish mining industry. The inventors patented their design and decided to charge mine owners a royalty. Cornish miners rebelled, setting up unauthorized adaptations of the original Watt machine.

In 1811, a group of leading miners founded the *Lean's Engine Reporter*, with a mission to collaborate and share ideas on new mining technologies and designs. This generosity and openness spurred innovation. Only a year after the journal was set up, two inventors, Arthur Woolf and Richard Trevithick, introduced a patent-free engine that became the standard. They allowed anyone to copy it. Watt and Boulton never made another sale, and Woolf and Trevithick made a killing installing and iterating on their original engine, fed, of course, by ideas that were circling around a community characterized by sharing.

Informal trading of knowledge can be found in certain pockets today. Engineers from rival firms often share problems they're working on and offer solutions. In the music industry, managers often share practices with one another. Lady Gaga's former manager, Troy Carter, told us, "With other managers, I'm extremely collaborative but also very competitive. We share information, problem-solve together. But I still want to beat them." Because the best practices in the music industry are changing, Carter says it's impossible to keep up without this kind of open exchange. "I'm one hundred percent okay with people copying. It's a situation where all boats rise with an idea."

You wouldn't expect to find the cooperative misfit instincts at work within traditional industries, but there is a strong tradition of cross-industry agreements. In the energy sector, it is common for companies to pool risk by going in together on upstream projects (searching for underground or underwater crude oil and natural gas fields, drilling, and operating wells). Shell will develop a field with Exxon, and their relative shares of production are proportionate to their equity stake in the project. Shell and Exxon jointly own the oil and production company Aera Energy, for example, with a 52 percent and 48 percent stake, respectively. Another type of joint venture can occur when one company takes the lead on project execution and the other assumes the role of "technology partner" to off-set some of the costs.

Some firms have endorsed collective innovation in R&D to help spread the costs of new technologies or materials. For example, Coca-Cola brought together a coalition of companies, including Ford, Heinz, Nike, and P&G, interested in sharing data and best practices around life-cycle assessment (a method for determining the environmental impacts of a product's life from cradle to grave). This collaboration emerged after Coca-Cola discovered that plant-based packaging was easier on the environment than traditional plastic bottles. Bottle for bottle, plant packaging was too expensive as a substitute, largely because there wasn't enough demand. Coca-Cola enlisted the support of other companies that could benefit from this approach, thereby increasing demand, stimulating supply, and reducing costs. The result was the Plant PET Technology Collaborative, the aim of which is to accelerate the development of 100 percent plant-based PET materials and fiber.

PATENTLY FALSE

Where do patents—originally conceived to enable entrepreneurs to recapture the time and money invested in bringing an idea to life—fit into the idea of copying as a strategy of the Misfit Economy? According to billionaire entrepreneur and investor Mark Cuban, the answer is nowhere. "Dumbass patents are crushing small businesses,"[15] he says.

Nathaniel Borenstein agrees. A computer scientist, Borenstein was part of the first wave of the open-source movement and developed email systems that could exchange multimedia messages. He sent the first email attachment on March 11, 1992. Borenstein went on to work for companies such as IBM and Mimecast. He explained: "Even where the misfits are successful innovators, they are usually bought out for a song by more sophisticated players." The patent system, he continued, "almost entirely works for the benefit of large corporations."

In 2012 IBM received 6,478 patents from the patent office, or one every eighteen minutes per workday.[16] Overall, between 1999 and 2008, the top 1.5 percent of patenting firms were responsible for 48 percent of all patents in the United States.[17] In contrast, most breakthrough innovations come from the little guy. Inventor Ronald Riley claims that "sixty percent of the National Inventor Hall of Fame inductees were selected for inventions that occurred while they were independent inventors, and not part of a corporation."[18]

Top economists at the St. Louis Federal Reserve published a paper in 2013 suggesting there is "no evidence" that patents improve productivity. They argue that patents can pose a threat to innovation.[19] Their policy solution? Patents should be abolished altogether. Perhaps it's about time. Debates around the value of patents and the nature and purpose of "claiming" intellectual property are nothing new. In the nineteenth century, many English anti-patent campaigners argued that innovation wasn't endowed to a "special breed of heroes" but to the everyman. They felt that the itch to invent was inborn.

In a nod to collective innovation, they didn't feel that any one inventor could or should claim credit or royalties when "there is no need to reward him who might be lucky enough to be the first to hit on the thing required."[20] Arriving at the invention of the steam engine or the cotton gin was attributed to right time, right place. If you hadn't done it, well, someone else would have. You just got there first.

It seems, then, that the patent system has always been an instrument of extraction, a collusion between the wealthy and their government. Historian Adrian Johns notes in his book *Piracy: The Intellectual Property Wars from Gutenberg to Gates* that these same anti-patent Englishmen felt that lower-class inventors were "hopeless in the face of big capital" due to the cost of patent fees, which in 1860 ranged from £100 to £120 (around $585), or approximately four times per capita income. The fee for a patent that also covered Scotland and Ireland could cost as much as £350 ($1,680). Renewing a patent could cost as much as £700 ($3,360).[21] While patenting was intended to "protect" the innovators, it brought high costs that only the wealthiest could pursue.

COPYING FOR THE GREATER GOOD

In many ways, intellectual-property pirates exist in response to the inequity of the patent system. They also exist as a counter-force to the monopoly of big business. Within the Misfit Economy, many feel that "ripping off" intellectual property is not only fair but morally justifiable.

As Jean-Phillippe Vergne, coauthor of *The Pirate Organization*, told us, "pirates emerge throughout history to challenge claims to monopolistic control." Vergne said that in the seventeenth century, the East India companies claimed rights on all the sea routes they had discovered. But after continued assault from sea pirates, the routes were declared "international waters."

Look at the ways in which radio pirates in the 1960s in Britain sought to bring an end to the BBC's domination of the airwaves by broadcasting their own content. Pirate radio stations broke the BBC's monopoly and forced BBC Radio to restructure and begin offering more diverse tunes. The BBC even went on to hire many pirate-radio DJs for their own stations.

One virtue of copycat innovators is that they can increase the pace of technological innovation and diffusion. In those areas where technologies or products are vital to the public good—such as essential medicines, alternative energy, or telecommunications—copycats can democratize vital products and services.

The success of generic pharmaceutical companies in India and Brazil provided multinational drug companies with real competition. At first these rivals could be found only in domestic markets, but as the manufacturers in India and Brazil scaled up and began exporting, they threatened the multinational companies' global market share.

India, for example, passed regulatory policies in the 1970s that allowed Indian companies to copy foreign patented drugs without paying a licensing fee. This law stimulated a local self-reliant pharmaceutical industry, as well as enabling more affordable medications. Patients could receive HIV/AIDS treatments that cost as little as $200 per year, compared to their name-brand counterparts at well over $10,000.[22]

Under new patent law that came into effect when India joined the WTO, Indian drug makers were no longer allowed to manufacture and market reverse-engineered versions of drugs patented by foreign drug producers. Many local pharmaceutical companies went underground. In pushing these players to the black market, quality control suffered. A lot of copycat medications simply didn't meet standards or didn't do what they claimed.

In contrast, in Brazil, the government retained much of its bargaining power and didn't force the copycat industry underground. Many essential drugs were regarded as "beyond patentable." In 2005 the Brazilian House of Representatives passed a bill that said HIV/AIDS medicines could not be patented.[23] Additionally, the same year, Brazil asked foreign pharmaceutical companies to license the generic production of their antiretrovirals for the country's STD/AIDS program.[24]

Germany, at the beginning of the twentieth century, did the same by restricting patents on essential goods. Akin to Brazil's stance in creating "unpatented domains" for essential medicines, Germany legislated that patents could not be obtained for food products, pharmaceuticals, or chemical products. The consequences resulted in "spurred productivity and diffusion in these industries."[25]

When it comes to innovations that have a direct bearing on the public good, open licensing—like what the Brazilian government enabled—has become the preferred course. It's not just governments mandating these approaches. Entrepreneurs and innovators are coming up with flexible licensing and open innovation schemes to enable the most vital innovations to scale.

HOW ILLEGAL DOWNLOADING INSPIRED INNOVATION

If you're like the many millions who download music, movies, and television shows, chances are you have frequented Netflix, the iTunes music store, Spotify, or Hulu. Maybe you've frequented all of them.

There is no question that legal music file-sharing programs like Pandora and Spotify are indebted to their illegal forefather, Napster, a program that exploited the vulnerabilities of the music industry and gave rise to a powerful alternative.

Storage services such as Dropbox and Google Drive owe to many illicit pirating sites like Megaupload. Moreover, much of the streaming video technology that now powers services like Netflix and Hulu is owing to the porn industry; porn websites were some of the first to embrace streaming technology.

Many gray-market innovations—whether streaming technology or file-sharing functionality—preceded more lucrative and legal business opportunities. In both the file-sharing and streaming markets, these platforms have transformed how the industry perceived entertainment content from something that users owned to something that they borrowed or rented. What the second wave of platforms (Hulu, Netflix, Pandora, and Spotify) enabled, however, was a sanctioned etiquette around file sharing.

Strict file-sharing sites had no way to reimburse content creators; hence the continuing outrage of many musicians, artists, and entertainment companies. After facing accusations that it was ripping off its artists, Pandora released figures suggesting that more than 2,000 of its artists would make $10,000 in the next year, while more than 800 were paid over $50,000. Popular artists like Adele, Coldplay, and Lil Wayne made over $1 million annually from the site.[26] By comparison, Spotify has paid out (as of November 2014) over $2 billion U.S. in royalties to the music industry since its launch in 2008.[27] The amount that each artist receives is based on his or her popularity.

Video-sharing companies like Hulu and Netflix have also stayed true to this etiquette, paying content providers through adapted business models built on revenue from subscription memberships. As of December 2013, Hulu had five million subscribers to Hulu Plus, its premium service, and was projected to reach $1 billion U.S. in revenue.[28] Meanwhile, Netflix has more than fifty million members worldwide[29] and has struck an exclusive three-year deal with Disney estimated at $300 million U.S.[30]

While these platforms use traditional licensing arrangements to compensate content providers, they also face competition from illegal file-sharing platforms. The irony is that businesses like Hulu and Spotify would have had a harder time getting off the ground if illegal file-sharing platforms hadn't disrupted the industry.

Some illegal websites that host pirated movies and television shows are still instrumental to the development and growth of the legal entities. When Netflix introduced service in the Netherlands, the company made clear that it used information from pirate websites to decide which shows and films to buy and offer. Kelly Merryman, the company's vice president of content acquisitions, told Tweakers, a Dutch website dedicated to covering all things tech: "With the purchase of series, we look at what does well on piracy sites."[31]

Artists are finding ways to beat the illegal downloading craze and evolving with the times. In the face of file-sharing politics, some artists have gotten creative. Rather than release a standard album, Beck released *Beck Hansen's Song Reader*, which consisted of sheet music rather than recorded songs. If fans want to hear it, they have to play it themselves. Such a step enables less passive consumption of content, as fans are given a role in bringing the music to life.

LETTING GOOD IDEAS SPREAD

In his book *Where Good Ideas Come From*, Steven Johnson states: "Protecting ideas from copycats and competitors also protects them from other ideas that might improve them [and] transform them . . . to true innovations."[32] Increasingly, misfit innovators are recognizing this and choosing to integrate copycat etiquette into the DNA of their own businesses.

Stephen Song, the founder of Village Telco,[33] subscribes to copying as "innovation for the public good." His company, which builds low-cost community telephone network hardware and software, aims to make starting a telephone company as easy as starting a blog. Song and his team designed the phone networking technology—which allows a phone company to be set up in minutes anywhere in the world, without the need for mobile phone towers or landlines—but refused to patent it. Instead, they gave the design to a manufacturer, who in turn agreed to produce the hardware cheaply and stay open to further design iteration by others.

By open-sourcing his technology, Song created what he calls "a fast track toward trust." Village Telco now has a network of more than five hundred people around the world who contribute to its technology faster than it could on its own. One user sought to customize the company to better serve local environments and small businesses. Now 30 percent of the community is using *his* version of the product rather than the original one.

Brazilian innovator Sergio Prado found a way to use patents for (public) good and not evil. "A patent is only a unit of information," Prado told us when describing how and why he has gone about patenting his process for creating construction materials out of waste. For Prado, patents are a way to package his solutions for greater scale. As he described, "Our objective is that the patent does not prevent the adoption of the innovation, but instead allows for immediate international collaboration to develop, test, and produce new building materials and housing applications at scale." Because Prado's patented solutions are for the public good—not only enabling reduced waste but also providing affordable housing—he allows for flexible licensing, encouraging others to make free use of his patented methods.

A similarly collaborative spirit underpins Copyleft, a form of licensing popularized in the open-source community, whereby a software program is put into the public domain with the condition that any use, modification, or redistribution of that program's code must also be put into the public domain. This requires programmers who build on a program to share their innovations with the original programmers and the community at large.

In the race to decode the cocoa genome, Howard-Yana Shapiro and his team took a similar tack. At confectionery manufacturer Mars Incorporated, Shapiro led the charge to sequence the genome, then put everything he'd learned into the public domain. He remembers the conversation in which he was granted permission lasting about five minutes: "I'd like to sequence the cocoa genome. I'll need six to eight million dollars to do it. And I want to give it away and put it in the public domain." And so it was.

Shapiro didn't stop there. Today he is working to sequence ninety-six orphan food crops. Orphan crops represent vital nutritional food crops for subsistence farmers across Africa,

Asia, and Latin America: cowpeas and mung beans (legumes), amaranth, sorghum, pearl millet, and teff (cereal grains). In his words, "These are poor people's crops; it doesn't make sense to hold on to the intellectual property." In addition to sequencing the crops, Shapiro is working with plant breeder networks in Africa to ensure that the crops can be distributed.

Some people think he is outright crazy; others fear that the scale of what he is trying to accomplish is too grand. However, Shapiro is on a mission to change the conversation—not only about sequencing but about the notion of intellectual property. "We gave away dominance of this commodity [cocoa] because it touches the livelihood of subsistence farmers. Why would we want to own it, defend it, and restrict its use when that could have negative consequences on people's livelihood?"

Similarly, Chas Bountra, another misfit whom we met, is trying to change pharmaceutical R&D. With over two decades of experience at GlaxoSmithKline, Bountra heads up the Structural Genomics Consortium at Oxford University. He is working on creating *pre-competitive* R&D.

Bountra is looking for investors and industry competitors to commit funds to develop new therapeutic targets. R&D budgets and targets are agreed upon and invested in; only when drugs reach Phase III trials will commercial sponsors be able to buy the drugs to bring them to market. Through this approach, Bountra hopes to bypass considerable R&D waste and redundancy. Currently, a pharmaceutical company will work on a therapeutic target that another may have found to be a dead end, but because the companies are competing, there is no incentive to share these dead ends: It is to one company's advantage to waste another's resources. Bountra's approach will create pre-competitive infrastructure that allows companies to cooperate on R&D while still competing to bring drugs to market.

Innovators like Bountra and Shapiro show us the importance of not being afraid to reach out to competitors to work on areas of shared vulnerability. Pre-competitive arrangements have historic precedent and may be needed now more than ever as core sectors of the economy—energy, pharma, and food—rethink their business models.

TIMING IS EVERYTHING

There are justifications for copying (good for business, good for humankind) when you are the copier. But what if you are the one being copied?

Eric Rosenbaum is one of the creators of MaKey MaKey, an "invention kit" that makes it easy to turn ordinary household objects into video game controllers (turn bananas into piano keys, create a joystick out of a pencil drawing). Eric and his business partner, Jay Silver, used Kickstarter to raise funds for their project. With an initial goal of $25,000, Rosenbaum and Silver ended up raising $568,106.

What makes this case study interesting is how two fringe cultures of innovation—the open-source culture and the shan-zhai culture of pirated innovation—collide. Through a strange series of events, Rosenbaum and Silver discovered a clone of their idea, called DemoHour, on a Chinese Kickstarter site. And the MaKey MaKey founders didn't like it.

It wasn't so much that the Chinese borrowed elements of their idea: MaKey MaKey is open-source, which means it is available for change and iteration. It was the way they went about it. The Chinese company relaunched the MaKey MaKey campaign word for word. They didn't differentiate from the MaKey MaKey product at all. And they hadn't attempted to contact Rosenbaum or Silver for permission. Nevertheless, the idea was a success in the Chinese market, as the Chinese company ended up raising over 326 percent of their fund-raising goal (or 16,346 yuan / $2,635 U.S.).

In this instance, there was a clear etiquette failure. If the Chinese copycats had contacted MaKey MaKey or sought to collaborate or even paid homage to the original innovators, it would have been a different story. Much copycat behavior boils down to etiquette. If you are learning and borrowing from others, it's important to acknowledge them.

Andrew Weinreich, a New York–based entrepreneur and creator of Six Degrees, one of the first social networking sites, has experienced being copied. Founded in 1996, Six Degrees was based on the popular idea (and Kevin Bacon game) that everyone is connected through six degrees of separation. Six Degrees essentially provided the ability to "see" people you didn't know through the network of people you did. What's interesting is that without photographs, all you would see was a list of friends in common.

While many of us are all too familiar with Facebook,

MySpace, and even Friendster, Six Degrees is a relative un-known. It wasn't a flop by any means. At its height, the site had more than a million users and a hundred employees. Its func-tionality was patented (now held by LinkedIn). In December 2000, Six Degrees was sold to Youthstream Media Networks for $125 million. A success by all accounts.

We asked Weinreich whether it upset him to see Six De-grees fade away, only to be replaced by other, wildly successful social networking sites. Did he resent Mark Zuckerberg and the success of Facebook?

"Absolutely not," Weinreich told us. "When people copy stuff that is contemporaneous, it is more upsetting than when they do it later." So time and space make copying easier to take. He added: "It's weird today to come up with an idea that nobody is doing."

Six Degrees was launched eight years before Facebook. At the time, the technology landscape was different. Weinreich told us how, when he was running Six Degrees, the top request from users was to be able to post a picture with a profile, but few had digital cameras. Camera phones didn't exist in the con-sumer market.

While it seems unimaginable now, Weinreich remembers thinking about what Six Degrees would need to provide for people to send in a physical photograph. His team would need to scan it and upload it to the site. "We were literally think-ing about the assembly line required for people to send in photographs. And then the dot-com bubble burst, and shortly thereafter we went from a world where there were no digital cameras to [a world where] everyone [had access to] digital photography."

In Weinreich's mind, Facebook never would have succeeded to the degree that it has without digital photography. (Facebook is the largest repository of photos in the world, with more than 250 billion photos, according to Mashable.[34]) Its superior execution over competitors like MySpace (which had a far less user-friendly interface) also mattered. That Facebook came along much later meant Weinreich was less bothered by the platform's success. While copying can be infuriating, it can play an essential role in hastening innovation.

It's important to remember that the person who comes up with an idea is not always the best person to execute it or see that idea scale up. If you are a creative sitting on a fountain of ideas, be sure to emphasize execution over ownership. Don't get caught up in a childish game of "mine." It isn't what you are able to think up or imagine but what you are able to do that matters. And if you are on the other side—the person taking someone's idea to the next level—then pay homage to the innovator. Flattery can go a long way.

IN EXPLORING THE WORLD OF MISFIT COPYCATS, WE HAVE SEEN VIRTUE IN the practice of copying. While we don't encourage or condone theft of intellectual property, we believe that there is great value in willingness to look to others for inspiration, and to build on their ideas with enhancements and improvements. We believe this form of collective innovation is intrinsic to the creative process and that this spirit should be harnessed in the formal economy, to accelerate the diffusion of innovation and to help avoid the establishment of monopolies.

We have observed the creativity of copycats who, without the burden of an emotional attachment to their inventions, have adapted their products to better suit the needs of their market. And we have learned that the success of an enterprise can be more a function of execution and timing than of having a brilliant original idea.

Chapter 4

HACK

SAM ROBERTS, A YOUNG ENGLISH HACKER, WAS BORN IN WHITBY, A SMALL seaside town in North Yorkshire, to parents with high expectations. His father was never a man to give praise easily; he encouraged Sam and his two competitive older brothers to "do better." Roberts's grandfather was, as far as he knew, the first person in the United Kingdom to build an electronic garage door (for his own purposes, not to commercialize it) by salvaging parts from an old washing machine. Later, the senior Roberts came up with an essential mining innovation, a safe electric cable that allowed miners to power forty-watt lights without causing a spark great enough to ignite gases. The queen of England honored him for this invention. And so whether explicitly, implicitly, or both, Sam Roberts got the message: With hard work and persistence, you could accomplish anything.

Roberts's pathway into hacking began after his ninth birthday. He received an electronics set as a gift, and with it, he configured a burglar alarm. After rigging the alarm up to his bedroom door, he took apart one of his walkie-talkies, wired the microphone to where the buzzer belonged on a burglar circuit, then connected other walkie-talkies around the house to notify him of any intruders. As a kid, Sam told us, he was obsessed with taking things apart. Toys, remote controls, radios, electric motors. He possessed a determination to know how everything worked because, he said, "that is the only way you can hack it, in order to make it do something different." Power and control also played a part in Sam's love of hacking. He told us he adored the feeling of knowing a system so well that he could manipulate it into doing whatever he commanded it to do. He was addicted, too, to the feeling of telling people that he had gotten access to something that most couldn't. When we asked him to describe the feeling, he began to tell us of the passion for magic that he developed as a kid: "Deception was awesome. I loved experiencing people's reactions to me doing something that seemed impossible. Hacking is very similar."

Roberts continued to hone his passion for building years later by studying electronics and communications engineering at the University of York. Following his graduation, he began to work first as a systems engineer, and then as a "white hat" hacker, helping to protect and strengthen government networks. His job entailed attacking government systems, finding vulnerabilities, and fixing them.

Roberts told us that, as a young boy and teenager, he became obsessed with learning everything he could about the process of breaking into a system. He bought a book, *The Anti Hacker Toolkit*, and worked through the chapters one by one. He learned how to hack into wireless networks, overcoming the security barriers set up by hotels and other establishments around Cheltenham, in Gloucestershire. He practiced by breaking into his roommates' computers (and telling them immediately afterward), finding a way to redirect their Internet traffic to his own computer.

At the age of twenty-five, he was itching to start his own company. He was introduced to a telecom director who gave Roberts a 2G mobile base station that he could take home. He studied the messages it sent and sent his own messages back until the system understood them. Once he grasped the crucial aspects of the protocol (which took him six months), Roberts developed a system that could control the base station and handle both mobile calls and SMS messages. He had built a mobile network from his own bedroom.

Today Sam Roberts is working with his brother Oliver on 4G mobile telecommunication network deployments throughout Europe, and continuing to embrace the hacker imperative: the driving need to understand how systems work and then put them back together in enhanced forms.

THE HACKER MOVEMENT

In his book *Hackers*, Steven Levy chronicles the birth and development of the hacker movement. He starts with the first iteration of hackers: the group who coalesced during the early 1960s, when the Massachusetts Institute of Technology (MIT) acquired its first programmable computer. This cohort's obsessive programming of the machines, and the relationship they built with the systems, gave rise to the Hacker Ethic, an informal, organically developed and agreed-upon manifesto that, in several iterations, still drives the hacker movement forward:

- Access to computers—and anything that might teach you something about the way the world works—should be unlimited and total.
- All information should be free.
- Mistrust authority—promote decentralization.
- Hackers should be judged by their hacking, not bogus criteria such as degrees, age, race, or position.
- You can create art and beauty on a computer.
- Computers can change your life for the better.

We found this ethic alive and well among the hackers we interviewed. When we asked why they hacked, we heard variations of "because of the thrill of commanding a computer to do what you design it to do." In fact, one of the meanings of the word "hacker," proposed by Eric S. Raymond in *The Jargon File* (a bible for hackers everywhere), is: "One who enjoys the intellectual challenge of creatively overcoming or circumventing limitations."

We spoke to several hackers acting under the banner of Anonymous who confirmed this motivation. Anonymous is, as described by anthropologist Gabriella Coleman, a "name employed by various groups of hackers, technologists, activists, human rights advocates, and geeks."[1] They appeared in newspapers worldwide when they took on the Church of Scientology, attacking and defacing the website after a video of Tom Cruise meant for internal promotion leaked to the public. Groups working under the Anonymous name then took on Aiplex, an Indian company contracted to take down illegal downloading websites like The Pirate Bay and those hosting the Motion Picture Association of America and the Recording Industry Association of America.

We spent over a year corresponding with a former member of Anonymous, who told us that his driving motivation to join the group was to get into systems that were not meant for his access. He said the moment he decided to join Anonymous was when he identified a cause that struck a chord with his view of the world. Because of his belief in open and free information, he began to take part in attacks against the companies trying to dismantle services like The Pirate Bay.

When we probed about his childhood, wondering why he became interested in hacking, he recalled getting home from school one day, turning his computer on, and realizing that it had been attacked by a virus. "I wanted to understand how something that I had not allowed in myself found its way onto my computer." He then became obsessed with understanding computers—how they're built, how they work, and how a human being can manipulate them.

He wrote to us about an incident of bullying at school, during which a classmate teased and tormented him. He went to the school principal, sure that resorting to authority would resolve the issues. The principal blamed him for putting himself in the position in the first place. He lost respect and trust for authority figures and stayed defiant in his wish to counter them and what they stood for. This played a big part in his decision to use computer systems to help the causes that challenged the authority he'd grown distrustful of. It became clear to us that a motivation for hacking was often a combination of the feeling you get when you solve a complex puzzle or riddle, a fundamental skepticism of authority, and the conviction that information should be freely available.

From Sam Roberts, and from the members of Anonymous, we found that hackers fervently believe in taking things apart in order to understand them. In this way, they can see not only the parts a system is composed of but also the connection between them. They are devoted to the perpetual improvement of systems; and in order to effectively improve something, they must have unfettered access to all information pertaining to that system. Without this free access, they believe that you can never really know how a system works from the inside. Naturally, this makes a hacker dedicated to getting his or her hands on information, and anything preventing that is viewed as an unwelcome obstacle.

While we were writing this book, news came through of the suicide of Aaron Swartz, a hacker, prolific builder, and warrior for the cause of open and free information. In his tragically short life—he was twenty-six—he cowrote at the age of fourteen the system for Real Simple Syndication (RSS), an innovation essential in the development of Google Reader, a technology that many once utilized every day. He was part of the Open Library, a platform that seeks to release, for free, one page of every book ever published. He cofounded Reddit, the hugely popular user-led news website. He was a feverishly dedicated soldier in the open-source/code/Web movement, contributing to the creation of the Creative Commons licensing. (As a countermeasure to copyright, Creative Commons is a license structure designed for creators of content to freely share their material, allowing others to legally build on the work.)

Later, Swartz was a general in the fight against Internet censorship, founding Demand Progress, a digital rights group that played a key role in defeating the Stop Online Piracy Act, a measure that sought to control which websites people could visit, proposed by Congress in 2012. His activism was fueled by the belief that all information necessary to make the world a better place should be free.

In 2008 he penned the Guerilla Open Access Manifesto, in which he clearly stated his beliefs:

We need to take information, wherever it is stored, make our copies and share them with the world. We need to take stuff that's out of copyright and add it to the archive. We need to buy secret databases and put them on the Web. We need to download scientific journals and upload them to file sharing networks. We need to fight for Guerilla Open Access.[2]

This explains the mission that would, sadly, consume him. In the quest to liberate information locked behind the paywalls of academic institutions, he began to download enormous troves of academic articles from JSTOR, a main host, through MIT's wireless network. When MIT noticed and blocked his wireless access, he sneaked in. He found his way to a network closet and plugged into the school's network. MIT discovered his operation, and in July 2011 he was charged by the U.S. attorney for Massachusetts with a potential sentence of thirty-five years in jail and $1 million in fines.

In January 2013, while awaiting prosecution for various alleged computer crimes, Swartz took his own life. We will never know exactly why. However, some of Swartz's family members have blamed the justice system and its intimidation tactics, saying, "Decisions made by the officials in the Massachusetts U.S. Attorney's office and at MIT contributed to his death. The U.S. Attorney's office pursued an exceptionally harsh array of charges, carrying potentially over 30 years in prison to punish an alleged crime that had no victims."[3] We may conclude that the prospect of being locked up, like the information Swartz so zealously sought to free, was anathema to his very being.

HACK 2.0

While the term "hacker" was traditionally used to refer to those like Sam Roberts, who toyed with computer systems, or Aaron Swartz, who fought to liberate information, the word has taken on broader connotations. We can say that Florence Nightingale hacked the medical profession by creating the vocation of nursing. Martin Luther King, Jr., hacked our political system to fight for civil rights. A child's mischievous selfie on a parent's cell phone is playfully captioned "Hacked!" A furniture painter who restyles an IKEA dresser to the point where it no longer resembles the ubiquitous Swedish brand dubs it "IKEA hack!" on Pinterest.

In recent years, the concept of hacking has continued to morph and spill over into mainstream organizations, with businesses hosting their own "hackathons," and words like "hack" and "disrupt" finding their place at the center of most future-friendly organizational cultures. These organizations have come to understand that hacking can both identify a system's weaknesses *and* see how it can be improved.

Within the Misfit Economy, the principle of hacking is about taking on the establishment to change it for the better. Hacking is also about getting to know a system intimately in order to more effectively take it apart. "Know your enemy" is an overused trope, but for good reason: There is tremendous power in understanding the system you are looking to reinvent.

EIGHTEENTH-CENTURY PIRATES AS HACKERS

"Every man shall have an equal vote in affairs of the moment." So begins the first article governing the pirate ship of Bartholomew Roberts ("Black Bart"), one of the most successful pirates of all time. Throughout his three-year career in the early eighteenth century, Roberts captured more than four hundred ships.[4]

What made such captains so successful? How did the pirate ships foster commitment, loyalty, and collaboration from a band of outlaws, rebels, and misfits? How did they establish the systems, rules, and order that helped to align and motivate their crews?

Pirates hacked the establishment. Computer hackers like Sam Roberts study a system, take it apart to understand every component, carefully identify its weaknesses, and then use the knowledge to build something new and improved. The pirates hacked the mainstream merchant ship system, the establishment from which most of them had originated.

Their lives on these merchant ships had been largely harsh and unforgiving. Merchant ship sailors sold their labor for money. They had no vote, they rarely were given a voice, and they had no ownership of the ventures. Their wages were low, too. Seamen on trading voyages were collecting less than twelve pounds (about twenty dollars) a year, while piracy offered a wage from a hundred to a thousand times more.[5]

On merchant ships, crewmen faced violent discipline at the hands of the captain, whose goal was to satisfy the interests of the land-based vessel owners. (The High Court of Admiralty records for this period are replete with bloody accounts of lashings, tortures, and killings.[6]) Merchant sailors often worked under a leader who enjoyed unlimited disciplinary power and a disturbing readiness to act on it.

It was the nature of life on board the merchant ships that inspired the pirates to take on the establishment, to hack it and change it for the better. As former merchant sailors, they knew the system, they were acutely aware of its weaknesses, and they understood from their own experiences how the hierarchical nature of the merchant ships left the crews feeling dissatisfied and disempowered.

Pirates used this knowledge to take the system apart and rebuild it in a completely different form. They turned upside down the world they knew and made the pirate ships everything that merchant ships were not; in so doing, they were able to create something that bound men in spirit, giving them a sense of purpose, passion, and a strong identification with the whole mission and values of piracy. "Pirates had a profound sense of community," writes Marcus Rediker; "they showed a recurring willingness to join forces at sea and in port, even when the various crews were strangers to each other."[7]

THE UNLIKELY DEMOCRATS

What did this hack look like? The world that the pirates created, the new order that turned the merchant ship system on its head, was based on principles such as shared ownership, equality, and democracy. Lurking behind the skull and cross-bones were men concerned with the health, wealth, and fair treatment of the majority. In hacking the establishment, they created a democratic system of self-governance that generated sufficient trust, order, and cooperation to make eighteenth-century pirate ships sophisticated, well-run, and successful organizations.

Based on the articles found on the ships of privateers and buccaneers (both early forms of pirates that were at times hired by governments to prey on enemy states), pirates wrote constitutions that served as their foundation of governance.

As described by Captain Charles Johnson, the "pirate journalist" of the time: "[Pirates] formed a set of articles, to be signed and sworn to . . . for the better conservation of their society, and doing justice to one another."[8] These constitutions were democratically formed and required unanimous agreement before any expedition set sail, allowing seafarers to decide whether they wanted to adopt them or go their separate ways.

This was extremely novel at the time. As Peter Leeson writes in *The Invisible Hook: The Hidden Economics of Pirates*, "It's truly remarkable to think that this model of democracy was staged not only on a pirate ship, of all places, but took place more than half a century before the Continental Congress approved the Declaration of Independence and only a little more than a decade after the British monarchy withheld Royal Assent for the last time."[9]

A pirate crew's captain or leader was democratically elected.

To separate power on the ship and prevent the misuse of authority, pirates created the office of the quartermaster, whose role was managing disciplinary issues, provisions, compensation for injury, bonuses for extraordinary effort, and appropriate punishments.[10]

The quartermaster was the most trusted member of the crew, but the most powerful office on the ship was the common council, a group composed of every single man on the ship. This council held an unrestricted right to depose both the captain and the quartermaster, with its decisions on all matters being sacrosanct.[11] Meetings were held regularly to decide on such matters as division of provisions, or on whether to attack or let a target be. Every pirate on board had a say in almost every decision that could impact the enterprise.

This reinvention of the hierarchy on merchant ships—this hack—meant that a crew was the real authority on a pirate ship. With the exception of battle, the ship's leader was just another voice among all others: "They only permit him to be captain," Charles Johnson commented, "on condition, that they may be captain over him."[12]

Peter Leeson and others write about the flat-pay structure, designed to diminish the material inequalities that could sink the enterprise. By more or less equally splitting seized treasure, pirates created motivated crews imbued with a sense of ownership, empowerment, and the willingness to continue in their plunder.[13] Centuries before socialists proclaimed the ills of unequal pay, centuries before the financial crisis exposed the grotesque salary gaps between Wall Street executives and regular employees and the potential social breakdown, pirates cracked the code: They understood that material inequalities would lead to a lack of trust, an unwillingness to collaborate toward one common goal, and in effect the inability to create a strong civic society. As Marcus Rediker wrote, "[Pirates'] painfully acquired experience told them that a fair distribution of risks would improve everyone's chance of survival."[14]

Pirates got other perks—the kind that drove collaboration. Their governance frameworks included income insurance for any man injured in battle, and bonuses to crewmen who displayed exceptional service. These incentives and social insurance schemes worked well. For the most part, crews on pirate ships did not deceive one another over the division of booty. Patrick Pringle, an author, attested to this: "I have not found a single case of a physical dispute during the share out or murders being committed to reduce the number of shareholders," he wrote in his book *Jolly Roger: The Story of the Great Age of Piracy*.

The nonhierarchical way of governing a pirate ship extended beyond compensation, a further reversal of the merchant ship system. In all aspects of life aboard a vessel, crewmen enjoyed the same social privileges as the captain and his officers. Captains faced deposition should they even try to secure a better way of life on board. Their lodging and provisions were typically the same as those of ordinary pirates.

By hacking the established merchant ship system, pirates built crews that were passionate, diligent, innovative, and highly committed, even during times of intense battle, when the men had to risk their lives in the name of the expedition's mission. Their governance structures managed to align the interests of these disparate groups of outlaws, ruffians, and rebels, turning them into cooperative and cohesive groups that were ruthlessly effective in their work, giving us one of history's most arresting periods: the golden age of piracy.

As mentioned earlier, Bartholomew Roberts's crew independently seized more than four hundred ships in just three years (1719 to 1722). Edward Teach, or "Blackbeard," captured roughly one hundred and twenty. "If we estimate that the remaining seventy or so pirate captains took an average of 20 vessels each . . . we would get a total of more than 2,400 vessels captured and plundered," wrote Marcus Rediker in his book *Villains of All Nations*. Considering these pirates were "in the market" under a decade, the numbers are pretty impressive.

Another way to measure their success is to determine the extent to which pirates' activity disrupted trade across the Atlantic. Rediker notes that there was "zero growth" in English shipping from 1715 to 1728, precisely the time when the most notorious pirates were most active. Captains and owners of merchant ships protested feverishly for their governments to take action to protect the seas and, as a result, their trade.

"The pirate," Rediker continues, "was thus a threat to property, the individual, society, the colony, the empire, the Crown, the nation, the world of nations, and indeed all mankind."[15]

Centuries before the invention of the computer, pirates successfully demonstrated the power of the hack, the potency of studying the establishment, taking apart the system to understand its every component, then using this knowledge to better it.

WHY HACK?

Today the characteristics associated with hackers are informing expectations around a new culture of work. Hackers pioneered many principles of informality that have since come to infect mainstream work culture. These include: problem-based work, a culture of openness and transparency, reputational and peer-based accountability (instead of rigid hierarchies and managers), and the permission to act on new opportunities.

In a letter to potential investors, Mark Zuckerberg of Facebook described the company's culture and unique management approach, which he dubbed "The Hacker Way."[16] "Hacking," Zuckerberg wrote, "is a means of building something or testing the boundaries of what can be done." He went on to describe hackers as people obsessed with continuous improvement and incessant iteration, believing that there is always room to do better and "that nothing is ever complete."

Hackers, too, attempt to build by "learning from smaller iterations rather than trying to get everything right all at once." Facebook has built a testing platform that allows employees to, at any given time, try thousands upon thousands of versions of Facebook's website. Wrote Zuckerberg: "We have the words

'Done is better than perfect' painted on our walls to remind ourselves to always keep chipping."

With Facebook claiming a hacker ethic, we can certainly see the risk of corporations who look to co-opt hacker sub-culture. But co-optation is only one of the ways in which the hacker movement is mainstreaming. A lot of the hacker ethic is still oriented around disruptive innovation and challenging the underlying logics and norms of the establishment, and these are the cases we're interested in—the hackers who are changing systems.

HACKING THE ESTABLISHMENT

Ivan Arreguín-Toft, an expert in asymmetric conflict, analyzed battles between larger armies and their smaller adversaries in his study "How the Weak Win Wars."[17] He found that in roughly 30 percent of these asymmetrical battles over the last two hundred years, the smaller, outnumbered army prevailed. For every one small-army soldier, the larger army had ten on average; however, the smaller armies often prevailed, as their leaders were—by virtue of their lesser size—better able to recognize a change in situation and quickly adjust their strategies. This remarkable statistic illustrates the value of being a hacker, a small and nimble agitator taking on the established incumbent.

A similar dynamic can be observed in the commercial world, where smaller players are adopting the hacker mindset, acting decisively to take on bigger, better-resourced, and highly established competitors; in doing so, they are disrupting industry after industry. Airbnb is disrupting the mammoth hotel industry. Spotify—and the wider wave of companies helping consumers experience music rather than own it—is forcing the music industry to change its business model. Car-lending and -sharing firms like Zipcar are inducing the automobile industry to rethink itself, suggesting a shift from selling cars to making them available without ownership.

Even drug-trafficking organizations and the contemporary Mafia have started to adopt a hacker's approach. As Moises Naim, the author and former editor of *Foreign Policy*, writes about the changing nature of the drug industry, "Rigid hierarchies in which authority is centralized don't do well in a high-speed global marketplace where opportunities and risks change too fast."[18] Naim goes on to point out how drug-dealing organizations have moved from hierarchical approaches to decentralized networks. In his words, "away from controlling leaders and toward multiple, loosely linked, dispersed agents and cells; away from rigid lines of control and exchange and toward constantly shifting transactions as opportunities dictate."[19]

Similarly, in an article for *Harvard Business Review*, Marc Goodman (formerly a police officer and counterterrorism consultant and now a cyber-risk and intelligence specialist) writes about the evolution of criminal organizations: "Modern organized crime has abandoned the top-heavy structure of dons, capos, and lieutenants made famous in *The Godfather*. Most of today's gangs, along with Al Qaeda and other terrorist groups, are loosely affiliated cooperative networks—and are as likely to recruit website designers and hackers as they are thugs and enforcers."[20]

THE PHYSICAL HACKERS

In the introduction, we profiled the group of physical hackers Urban eXperiment (the UX), which undertakes clandestine work in the depths of Paris. The UX are not computer hackers, but they pay heed to the Hacker Ethic: They build, take apart, and restore physical objects in the same way a computer hacker would a program.

The UX is made up of French men and women who have "aboveground" duties of work and family but adopt different personas (even fake names) and go underground in order to fulfill a mission that Jon Lackman, a writer and art historian, described as tending to "the black sheep: the odd, the unloved, the forgotten artifacts of French civilization."[21]

The group is perhaps best known for the audacious act of breaking into one of France's most sacred buildings, the Panthéon (which hosts the remains of figures like Voltaire, Victor Hugo, and Émile Zola), in 2006. The UX's mission, once inside, was to remain undetected while repairing a neglected nineteenth-century clock. Without being noticed by alarms or security guards, the UX wired a concealed room for electricity, Internet, and a fridge, and smuggled in the tools necessary to get the job done. Over the course of a year, the group restored the Panthéon's clock, which had been awaiting a restoration promised by the French state since the 1960s.

While not being formally acknowledged as "experts," the UX has built an extensive record on practices ranging from infiltration to restoration. Their knowledge, particularly of the city's vast and complex tunnel system, allows them to gain access to places that even French authorities struggle to penetrate.

As with the informal, loose codification of the Hacker Ethic, the UX has no manifesto, only the desire to gather knowledge through constant experimentation. Jon Lackman expressed it to us this way: "In French, the word 'experience' can mean both 'experience' (as in living through an occurrence) and 'experiment.'" Members of the UX aim for each project to be a rewarding experience, but as with an experiment, they also seek to learn something about how the world works. Like the hackers we introduced earlier in this chapter, the UX thrives on the motivation to become experts in a system. The experiments on the system can reveal lessons, each building on the previous one. "But an experiment cannot live on by itself," Lazar Kunstmann told us. For innovation to thrive, an organization must have the ability to continue asking questions, and for the UX, projects need to be worked on constantly or they die.

Their structure lends itself to the eternal state of probing curiosity. While every activity the UX undertakes has a sense of order, the group has separate cells dedicated to different disciplines (one for accumulating knowledge and tactics on infiltration of key passages and buildings; others for the running of film and art festivals), it is entirely informal as a whole: "Anyone can come and go freely from project to project, cell to cell, or swap roles." A member who is part of the infiltration island can easily cross over to the one dedicated to organizing film festivals, bringing about a fusion of ideas and perspectives.

Like computer hackers, the UX zealously adheres to the practice of logging every single project, activity, success, and failure into an ever-expanding database. Kunstmann, when probed about this practice, told us about the conquistadores who first arrived in South America. One of the primary reasons for their successes in battle, he said, was that they had access to a gargantuan military library: "They knew every trick in the book." Taking their lead from the conquistadores, members of the UX build knowledge within their community through recording their experiences and via the free flow of this information within the group.

The UX embodies the hacker mentality. They take on the establishment, not just to satisfy an urge to fix and improve but also for the betterment of society. Like the eighteenth-century pirates and modern computer hackers, they seek to do so by developing an intimate understanding of the system that they wish to improve so they can effectively rebuild it.

Perhaps most important, the UX operates stealthily through the underground tunnel system. Any hacker must know how to avoid detection and must work to not get spat out by institutional antibodies. Camouflage isn't a strategy just for the devious but for those who may need their work to stay under the radar until they have the right buy-in and support.

A RELUCTANT HACKER,
A LATE-BLOOMING MISFIT

Gary Slutkin, M.D., was never a misfit. A physician by training, a "very conventional training," he added, Dr. Slutkin had
devoted himself to designing behavior change and epidemic
control programs. As a chief resident at the prestigious San
Francisco General Hospital, Slutkin worked on a tuberculosis
prevention program. After two years, new cases of TB infec-
tion in the surrounding area dropped by over 50 percent, and
the rate of those completing TB therapy increased from 50 to
95 percent.

Next stop was Somalia. When Slutkin told his mentor at
San Francisco General Hospital where he was going, his mentor told him it was the biggest mistake he could ever make, that
he was jeopardizing his career.

In Somalia, Slutkin worked for the country's director of
primary health care and assisted in preventing the spread of
tuberculosis and a deadly cholera outbreak. He landed in the
middle of a dire situation, with more than a million refugees
occupying forty camps. Because his team had limited resources,
they ended up recruiting and training refugees to become spe-
cialized health workers. Similar to Florence Nightingale's introduction of the nursing profession, this approach introduced
a new category of worker into health systems: the indigenous
worker who already had the access and trust of the local population.

After three years in Somalia, Slutkin took a position at the

World Health Organization, where he worked to fight the HIV/AIDS epidemic in Uganda. Overall, Slutkin spent nearly ten years in fifteen countries in Africa and Europe as a major leader in the battle against infectious disease.

His personal life and professional life suffered. After ten years on high alert, he was exhausted, physically and mentally, and feeling emotionally isolated. But he was gratified to see extraordinary breakthroughs.

He returned to the United States and soon found himself asking, "What next?" He started hearing about kids shooting each other. "I was reading these horrific stories of ten- and twelve-year-old kids killing each other in the streets, and I asked people what was being done about it." It was a simple question, one that might be posed by any concerned citizen. But it was a question that Slutkin would spend the next fifteen years attempting to answer.

Slutkin was stunned and disappointed by the so-called solutions that existed for treating violence. "We knew that punishment wasn't a main driver of behavior," he told us. "This was a problem that was stuck." Discouraged, Slutkin began to study patterns of violent outbreaks and made a startling observation: Violence spreads much like infectious disease. "What I saw in the maps of violence I studied was characteristic clustering—just like the maps that I had seen in other epidemics, such as cholera." That was Slutkin's "aha moment." "I thought, what if we started treating violence as a contagion?"

One of the biggest and most insidious plagues on our society is violence. Yet too often the discourse focuses on labeling the violent individuals as deviants or "evil." What if, Slutkin wondered, we removed the labels and the judgment and began to treat violence objectively—like a disease that is transmitted and spread, much like the common cold? He joked, "You can't even see bad under the microscope. There is no place in science for the concept of bad or the concept of enemy."

His leap from A to B was slow. It took him about five years to reframe the problem of violence in his own mind. He lost himself in debate and discussions about the drivers of violence. He read all the latest reports and white papers. He became obsessed with the topic and with the ways he thought he could bring a "cure" to the world. This kind of obsessive knowledge of the system you're trying to fix is essential for any hacker. You need to understand the rules in order to know how to break them or pioneer something different. Having one foot in the system you're trying to change, and one foot outside to maintain perspective, allows you to maintain an insider/outsider mind-set and approach.

Slutkin's background in health and his immersion in the field of violence prevention allowed him a unique vantage point to see through the bias of the system. For example, a lot of existing practice focused on punishment as a solution to violence, but based on his work in the health field, Slutkin knew punishment was never used as a tool for behavior change. A lot of those who advocated punishment reminded Slutkin of a historic period in epidemic history when people didn't have an understanding of diseases and thought things like plague, leprosy, and smallpox were caused by bad people or "bad humors." Slutkin told us how these misunderstandings often led people to blame, exclude, and punish the victim of disease, which caused additional suffering.

Seeing violence outside a moralistic lens required a radically different approach. But compounding systemic problems of poverty, racism, drugs, and other chronic issues impacting violent communities wasn't efficient or actionable. Even choosing to work with political systems to regulate gun control could take decades and hadn't seen much success to date, at least in the United States. So rather than wait for a magical silver-bullet solution, Slutkin realized he could help stop the spread of violence, in much the same way that he had stopped the spread of disease in Somalia.

From there, Slutkin's organization, Cure Violence, was framed around a simple hypothesis: The most critical thing is to disrupt the transmission of violence.

Slutkin then developed a community role for "violence interrupters": outreach workers called in to delicate situations where violence could occur, much like the community outreach workers he employed in the refugee camps. So if people in a particular neighborhood hear about a potential retaliatory shooting or a conflict brewing between gangs, they can call in violence interrupters, who go into the neighborhood and attempt to prevent the violence from being transmitted.

For example, a mom in Chicago discovered that her teenage son was loading weapons with his friends in their house. She was frantic and didn't know what to do because it was her son and his friends, and she wasn't going to call the police on her kid. But she needed someone to do something. So she called Cure Violence, and they sent over a few interrupters to talk to the teenagers. Over the course of a few hours, they were able to calm the group of kids. The interrupters know how to buy time and allow people to cool down; most important, they listen. A lot of their method is about the art of persuasion.

These interrupters are often from the communities where the violent outbreaks are occurring. Many of them have been in prison or had their own experiences with violence. As a result, communities trust and believe in them, which allows them to be much more effective than the police force.

One violence interrupter Slutkin told us about was working with a group preparing for a revenge killing when he got a call about another conflict building nearby. He asked the first set of guys to go over and help him with the other group. He solicited their advice in getting the second group to calm down. He got their minds totally fixed on helping the second group— and forgetting about their own problems. In employing them to help with the second group and listen to their problems, he also got them to disassociate from what they were dealing with and adopt a different perspective.

Another intervention by Cure Violence related to a teenager who was hiding out in the basement of his parents' house in Chicago because a peer had told him that he would be killed if he went back to school. He hid in the basement for six months. His parents finally called a violence interrupter, who went into the school and called in a favor from the student who had issued the threat. Because the interrupters have community credibility, access, and trust, they can be powerful mechanisms of persuasion in these situations.

The year Cure Violence was implemented, the West Garfield neighborhood of Chicago saw a 67 percent drop in shootings, while comparable areas saw a reduction of 20 percent. In fact, there were long stretches of time—as long as ninety days—without any shootings, which was previously unheard of. With the help of a senator from Illinois, Cure Violence was able to scale up to other neighborhoods. These communities showed a 42 percent drop in shootings in the first year, with comparable areas experiencing only a 15 percent reduction.

Fifteen years later, Slutkin is leading the charge to transform how we diagnose and treat violence. Cure Violence is scaling up across the United States, now operating in twenty-two cities. New York City recently announced that it plans to invest $12.7 million to roll out the program. And Slutkin's methods are being used not just in the United States but also in places like Iraq, where Cure Violence has interrupted more than 500 incidents of violence to date.

Cure Violence has reduced killings by up to 56 percent and shootings by 44 percent in communities where it operates. The organization is also changing the norms around violence. In communities where Cure Violence has a presence, people are four times more likely to show little or no support for gun use.

Mainstreaming this misfit approach to violence wasn't easy. "I never thought there would be pushback," Slutkin told us. "We were never trying to cause a disruption or hack a system. I'm not coming from that background. All that I was doing from a health perspective was trying to design something that filled an obvious gap. In health, everyone wants a better treatment. But working with violence, what surprised me was that people found that this was disruptive and threatening. And that's when I started feeling like more of a hacker."

Slutkin told us that Cure Violence faced pushback from federal agencies, academia, law enforcement, prison systems, and competitors working on violence reduction. Because Slutkin didn't have a background in violence prevention, he was dismissed. "I wasn't part of the club," he told us. "So many of the initial proposals I put together were rejected." If you are hacking a system from the outside, it's often important to build allies within the system who can champion your cause. This is something Slutkin learned with time.

Another big issue with the solution was a moralistic mindset. "The idea that those who commit violence aren't bad really disrupts people's ideas. So many actors are addicted to this good-guy-versus-bad-guy script. And a lot of the press is in the same realm."

What has allowed Slutkin to be successful is focusing on continuously getting results. The science keeps getting better and better, he told us. It is becoming more recognized that violence is a contagious process. That is helping people realize that you "can't arrest and imprison your way out of this problem," Slutkin said.

Over time, Slutkin has been able to provide an alternative to how we go about treating violence. He hacked the system by challenging entrenched views on violence and its perpetuators;

he then prototyped a solution for how to end violence. His network of violence interrupters are the "hack" that he wants the system to adopt.

The success of hacks like Slutkin's depend on experimentation—the capacity for improvisation—as well as the ability to infect the mainstream or package your "hack" so that it can be embedded into the rules and norms of the establishment.

Slutkin is trying to get his solution adopted by local governments, police forces, and community outreach networks. But Cure Violence doesn't scale through strict replication. Rather, the organization builds partnerships with city groups and other organizations to transfer their methods. They apply more open-source principles for spreading their methods, and host training initiatives to share their learning.

In this way, Slutkin embodies the hacker mind-set, believing that Cure Violence's methods should be open and available to all, with an invitation to make your own improvements. In hacking, nothing is ever the end product. With the conviction that a system can always be improved upon, hackers see their projects as living organisms that, without attention and constant work, will die. Cure Violence is perfectly aligned with this approach. "It's a bit like an open-source network," Slutkin told us. "The intervention is not complete—it needs to continue to evolve. We keep tweaking the model and making it more powerful and effective and create a network where learning can be shared."

When we asked Slutkin what his strategy has been for hacking the system, he confessed that he isn't an aggressive hacker. "I don't like fighting," he said. "I avoid naysayers and let the results of the program speak for itself. Over time, we're finding that more people are able to speak for this movement." For example, justice departments are now spreading the word. And Slutkin hopes that international organizations like the World Health Organization will begin talking more about violence as a contagion and seeing it as a health issue. "For this solution to really tip, we need the health sector to step up and explain it: to say that a lot of violent behaviors are acquired unconsciously; that they are addictive, just like smoking."

In the future, Slutkin imagines that every health department will have a robust violence reduction unit, that these units will work with select community organizations to dispatch networks of interrupters and that these networks will be coordinated with hospitals. So when you see patients in the emergency rooms, there will be regular dispatching to prevent retaliation and effectively treat those who have been wounded. "Not just treat their wounds," Slutkin says, "but treat them psychologically, so when they leave the hospital, they aren't at risk of spreading and transmitting violence on the streets."

THE HACKER MENTALITY RUNS STRONGLY THROUGHOUT THE MISFIT ECONOMY: A burning desire to take on the establishment. A commitment to the free sharing of information, which can enable collaborative innovation. An itch to fix or improve. An aspiration to gain a deep understanding of a system (and all its components) so it can be rebuilt or enhanced. These are all principles that can be applied to great effect in the formal economy, as we seek to improve the organizations, the systems, and the institutions that surround us.

Chapter 5

⚔

PROVOKE

IMAGINE A TWELVE-YEAR-OLD ASKING: "WHAT IF WE DIDN'T HAVE TO GO TO school?"

Okay, maybe it's not so hard to imagine a twelve-year-old asking that question. But what if it were a philosophical query that provoked real change in the way people valued and structured education?

At age twelve, Dale Stephens wondered just that. Frustrated with the classroom setting, Stephens decided to leave school and dove headfirst into "unschooling." Unschooling is a type of homeschooling that emphasizes real-world learning experiences over text-driven classroom learning, a student-directed "curriculum" over teacher- or government-dictated mandates. While his peers attended traditional middle and high schools,

Stephens started businesses, lived abroad, worked on political campaigns, and helped build a library.

In 2011 Stephens founded UnCollege, giving himself the job title "chief educational deviant." UnCollege provides resources to students who wish to avail themselves of educational opportunities beyond the domain of traditional higher education, like colleges and universities. Inspired by his personal experience with unschooling and his frustrations with the college experience (for a short time, he attended Hendrix College in Arkansas), Stephens says that the goal of UnCollege is *not* to convince people not to go to college but to shine a light on educational alternatives—and to encourage more people to consider the opportunity cost of attending a traditional institution of higher learning.

As a kid, Stephens had the wherewithal to seek out mentors who could teach him what he wanted to learn. When he was fourteen, Stephens learned that a friend's parent was a writer, so he asked if she would mentor him. For a few years she did, until Stephens's writing improved and he felt confident going it alone. Stephens also took classes that he and other unschoolers organized themselves, around topics that interested them. "It was great [in contrast to] when I was in school, [and] I remember thinking, 'Why should I spend seven hours a day dealing with teachers and students who didn't really want to be there?' It was a waste of time."

In assuming responsibility for his education, Stephens feels that he learned valuable soft skills often overlooked in traditional classrooms. "I was able to develop more meta-skills rather than just [be exposed to] subject matter. While I learned math and history, I also learned about how to evaluate myself, how to find mentors, and how to set goals. And, most importantly, how to be self-aware. All sorts of things that nobody was bothering to teach me when I was in school."

At sixteen, Stephens decided he wanted to get more involved in start-ups and technology. His first job was at a tech company, working alongside a group of college dropouts from Princeton who sought to match students with colleges. "It was a bit funny, because we were all dropouts funneling people into the educational system. But I learned a lot."

Despite his success, Stephens is surprised by the extent to which he has to defend his decision to leave school. "I've had to argue my case every day since I left. When I say 'I'm gay,' nobody is like 'Oh, have you considered being straight?' But they do say 'Oh, what if you had stayed in school?'"

The unschooling movement may be a niche, but alternative education is a growing marketplace. "Our education system was used to make industrial workers out of agricultural workers. It is no longer adequate," Howard Rheingold told us. Rheingold, sixty-seven, is the former editor of *Whole Earth Review*. Founded in 1985, *Whole Earth Review* was a countercultural publication evolving out of Stewart Brand's *Whole Earth Catalog* and rooted in "that old American tradition of self-reliance," Rheingold shared, "building on that misfit streak started by Emerson." In Rheingold's perspective, *Whole Earth Review* was all about sharing tools and ideas to get people to take more control over their lives. "There was this hope that you didn't have to depend on distant institutions—government, business, religious organizations—to shape your life." Many came to realize that it was impossible to live completely outside of American society. *Whole Earth* wasn't a solution but an ideal. It was a provocation for Americans to tap into greater self-reliance, to become makers and craftsmen.

Today Rheingold is part of Dale Stephens's mission to reimagine our educational systems along similar lines of self-reliance and autonomy. "School is largely about compliance," he told us, "sitting in your desk and keeping quiet." Rheingold is working to develop models of peer education in which students are no longer passive consumers of content but are able to co-learn with each other. It is provoking a similar ideal to *Whole Earth*, with the message "Take charge of your life; don't depend on formal (educational) institutions, but do it yourself."

Howard Rheingold, Kio Stark, and Dale Stephens belong to a tribe of misfits who are *provoking* the education conversation: questioning dogmas and assumptions about how we learn and how we teach, and pioneering different approaches to education. As Rheingold told us, "We are in an era of extremely rapid change. What works today won't work tomorrow. We are going to need misfits for society to find its way. Misfits who can point out tomorrow."

THE POWER OF PROVOCATION

To provoke, of course, means to arouse or stir up feelings, desires, or action. Within the Misfit Economy, provocation is about stepping out of reality, imagining something different. It is about poking and prodding business as usual to get others to wake up to different possibilities, just as Dale Stephens did.

The principle of provoke isn't about having all the answers or even any of the answers. It's about creating the conditions for a new conversation to take place, challenging orthodoxies, encouraging dissent, and imagining alternatives.

Ultimately, provocation is about learning to harness your own self-expression to take a stand and shake up the status quo. This skill is important for anyone—manager, spouse, parent, entrepreneur—who may not be a political agitator but may feel "stirred up" to take a stand within a company, marriage, school district, or start-up. To challenge "the way we've always done things" and make room for something new.

In an age of sexual prudishness, Helena Wright challenged women to think about sex as a pleasurable activity beyond reproduction. Writers Edgar Allan Poe and Jules Verne got us to think about the feasibility of space flight. Jane Austen called our ideas of marriage into question through her romantic fiction. Rosa Parks challenged norms around segregation by refusing to give up her seat on the bus. Coco Chanel pushed the boundaries of women's fashion and never hesitated to speak her mind ("The most courageous act is to still think for yourself, aloud," she once said).

Artists and writers, protestors and social reformers, misfits all. But call them what they are: successful. Like all great entrepreneurs, misfit provocateurs make us believe in a different version of the truth because they have the audacity to imagine a different world.

EXPLORING NEW WORLDS

Artist Angelo Vermeulen told us that he never expected to become a commander for a NASA space mission. In April 2013 Vermeulen (who also has a Ph.D. in biology) became a crew commander for HI-SEAS, a space mission simulation intended to re-create the experience of living on Mars. For four months Vermeulen lived with five other people in a simulated space station on the volcanic soils of Hawaii.

Funded by NASA, the mission was set up primarily to explore how to offer nutritional food to astronauts during long periods of isolation. The experiment also offered insights into crew structure, leadership, and community building in cramped quarters.

Vermeulen told us that at times the simulation felt incredibly real, like living on Mars. Whenever the crew took part in extra-vehicular activities, for example, they wore space suits to leave the station. But other days, "when you are homesick or you have a difficult moment, you step out of the illusion and realize you are just on a volcano in Hawaii," Vermeulen said. It was important for the well-being of the crew to maintain the simulated reality. "The closer you get to the feeling of really being on a mission, the more you enjoy it."

The Mars simulation is similar to many live-action role-playing games (known as LARPs). Though LARP is a misfit subculture often associated with nerds running around with swords in the woods, it is being used increasingly as an experimental artistic medium to explore alternative worlds. There have been LARPs set up to explore important themes, including refugee camps, prisons, AIDS, homelessness, and gender roles. The game Motherland was a LARP set up as an alternative history in which Germany had won World War II. Another LARP organized in Sweden was built around the premise of a fictional girl who had been kidnapped. This LARP used online and offline elements, mixing a TV series and an Internet platform that enticed players on a real-life scavenger hunt to find the missing girl.

LARPs can allow players to experience particular emotions, step into another's perspective, and explore artistic and political visions that might not be part of mainstream culture. LARPers build temporal realities that one can explore and learn from. LARPers call it "bleeding" when what you feel or learn within a game moves into your everyday life.

In some ways, the Mars simulation was an extended LARP. While crew members got to be themselves, they had to pretend to be living on Mars, and often it was hard not to break the simulation. To cope with the intensity of being trapped in relatively cramped quarters, some crew members would listen to music from their teenage years or play video games or even think about holiday plans for after the four-month mission. To keep up the illusion, Vermeulen worked to create a temporary structure. The crew would have a schedule, with morning meetings and chores. He tried to promote a lot of interaction, too, so the crew would feel more like a makeshift family.

The crew was being studied by NASA scientists who were interested not only in food strategies for living in space but also in the psychological implications of that kind of isolation. The crew's correspondence with the outside world was studied to see if triggers could be found in communication that indicated certain psychological tendencies or states of well-being.

As Vermeulen told us, "We were not really aware of what exactly NASA was learning or what came out of it." The mission generated a lot of press, and in turn, that made the idea of living on Mars a little more tangible for people. "The idea of how to feed your astronauts and keep them healthy touches a nerve for people," Vermeulen said. "Grounding outer space in a discussion of the food reality makes it seem realistic and like not such a distant future." Ultimately, the experiment was more of a provocation than an intensive research expedition.

As an artist with a background in the sciences, Vermeulen uses art as a way of probing into possible futures. He explores space colonization through art. Another project he is involved with is around starship design. Called Seeker, the project brings together volunteers to design the interior of a spaceship. The spaceship travels around the world, and new groups of people reconstruct its interior to fit their needs or experiment with different building materials. As with the Mars simulation, Vermeulen started running his own "isolation missions" in the fabricated starships. At the Museum of Modern Art in Ljubljana,

Slovenia, Vermeulen spent four days with five other volunteers inside the starship, where they discussed interstellar voyaging and experienced what it was like to live in a starship of their own design.

Seeker is a community-designed art project that allows people to experience and reimagine the future of human habitation. Vermeulen admitted that part of his penchant for starship design owes to science fiction and the space architecture you see in shows like *Battlestar Galactica*. "It isn't just engineers who drive research possibilities. It is artists as well." Vermeulen's background in biology allows him to do architectural modeling for starships that mimic biological structures and systems; his art uses biology and computer simulations to generate speculative designs. "It's this hybrid identity, as an artist and researcher—or a researcher through the arts—that is the driving force of my work."

THE USE OF ART TO PUSH THE BOUNDARIES OF THE PUBLIC IMAGINATION around space is nothing new. In 1835 Edgar Allan Poe penned a short story called "The Unparalleled Adventure of One Hans Pfaall" that told the story of one man's journey to the moon using hot-air-balloon technology. The story was one of Poe's lesser-known writings and didn't draw too much attention. Dissatisfied, Poe put on his con-man hat and published a fictitious news article in 1844 in the *New York Sun* (a politically conservative newspaper) about a man who traveled the Atlantic Ocean by hot-air balloon in only three days. The newspaper article was later revealed as a hoax and retracted. But before the story was discredited, it proved quite popular. Poe had described the mechanics of propulsion in great detail and had excited—through his deceitful shock-and-awe tactics—the popular imagination.

Both of Poe's stories would later influence Jules Verne's novel *From the Earth to the Moon* (1865). In turn, Verne's story went on to inspire many early space flight pioneers. Konstantin Tsiolkovsky was a Russian schoolteacher influenced by Verne's novel. Verne's story is full of calculations around space flight. Engaging with Verne's text, Tsiolkovsky went on to show that space flight was possible. He rightly predicted that liquid fuel rockets would be needed to get people to space and that hydrogen and oxygen would be the most powerful fuel. Robert Goddard was another space flight pioneer who, as a teenager, was influenced by reading Verne as well as H. G. Wells's *The War of the Worlds* (1897). Goddard launched the world's first liquid-fueled rocket in 1926 and earned more than two hundred patents for his work in space flight.

In speaking with economist Alexander MacDonald, who works at NASA's Jet Propulsion Laboratory, we came to appreciate the influence of science fiction in provoking the scientific imagination around space flight. "Many people who work at NASA are inspired and motivated to do what they do because of the influence of science fiction in their lives." MacDonald told us that many of his colleagues at NASA have taken part in science fiction communities; many have even penned novels. "Science fiction writers are versed in the more technical aspects of space flight, and so there is a lot of exchange and inspiration that flows between NASA scientists and writers." MacDonald told us that science fiction writers are sometimes invited to speak at NASA conferences.

Science fiction author and blogger Cory Doctorow, for example, published a novella for Project Hieroglyph, a platform for science fiction stories. Doctorow wrote about maker-space hardware hackers and Burning Man devotees who build 3-D printing robots to send to the moon. Accompanying the story, Hieroglyph hosts on their website a discussion with scientists around the feasibility of 3-D printing on the moon. Hieroglyph is a matchmaker of sorts, encouraging the conversion of science fiction stories into reality. The name comes from the recognition that certain stories serve as "hieroglyphs" or symbols—like Isaac Asimov's robot—that activate the minds of engineers, entrepreneurs, and scientists around how an innovation can come to be. In other words, the platform fosters an appetite among innovators to bring science fiction "hieroglyphs" into reality.

When astronaut Neil Armstrong returned from the moon as part of the Apollo 11 expedition, he referenced Verne's novel in a television broadcast before reflecting on his own time in space. Without Poe and Verne creating the imaginative possibility of traveling to the moon, Armstrong might never have gone. In this way, art is a powerful tool in opening up our consciousness to new possibilities. In Edgar Allan Poe's showing how space flight could work, or Vermeulen's conceiving how life on a Mars space colony or in a starship could be, a writer and an artist opened doors for scientific discovery. They were provocateurs of the public imagination. Their influence may be difficult to trace and parse out, but it's also undeniable.

INSIDE A MOUNTAIN IN WESTERN TEXAS, A TEN-THOUSAND-YEAR CLOCK IS currently being built out of stainless steel and titanium by a group of artists and engineers. The clock will be hundreds of feet tall and designed to tick for ten thousand years, approximately the length of our civilization at present.

We spoke to Alexander Rose, the "project manager" for this ambitious undertaking. Rose, who grew up in a junkyard in Sausalito, where he honed his passion for tinkering, told us that the purpose of the clock is to "create an icon for long-term thinking that can inspire us to solve problems with long time spans." At the moment, Rose feels that with many of the problems we go after, we look for solutions that pay off within a few years. "But so many of the problems we face—from climate change to environmental collapse—are not problems created overnight, nor problems that will take just a few years to fix."

As much as the clock poses an engineering challenge, Rose sees the project as more of a provocation in the spirit of art or theater, to get people to challenge their established time scales. "We are trying to change the conversation people are having. Designing an experience that people move through and are affected by, like theater." The clock is being built to capture people's attention; its size is part of this strategy. Rose tells us that the clock must be designed to impress people so they'll tell stories about it. "New myths are being created," he told us. "People are being given permission to think about things at a longer scale."

The ten-thousand-year clock shows how certain short-term ways of thinking are misguided or broken. It asks us to change our assumptions about time. And this is the essence of the provocateur experiment—the ability to completely redefine assumptions, to ignore the status quo and mentalities that say, "This is how we've always done it." In provoking, we can't be afraid to simply ask, "Why?"

When considering how and why to provoke, remember that provocation doesn't usually lead to a direct cause-and-effect change, right here, right now. When you are provoking, you aren't tied to a specific outcome. You are taking a stand—and you aren't always aware of the consequences.

BEARDS OF PROTEST

La Barbe is a group of French feminists. Its activists wear fake beards and storm male-dominated events to denounce the underrepresentation of women. They were inspired by Guerrilla Girls, a New York City–based feminist group of artists who donned gorilla masks in 1985 to protest the lack of gender diversity at the Museum of Modern Art. In March 2008, at one of La Barbe's first public events, the group showed up in Paris on International Women's Day to glue a beard on one of the statues in Republic Square. Since then, the group has staged somewhere between 150 and 200 interventions. La Barbe has provoked a response at many male gatherings, from political conventions to business board meetings. But one of the most notable was during the Cannes Film Festival.

On May 12, 2012, La Barbe gained attention by having one of their opposition pieces run in *Le Monde*, entitled "In Cannes, Women Show Their Reels, Men, Their Films." The piece brought attention to the fact that the twenty-two films in the official selection of the Cannes Film Festival had been made by twenty-two men. The content was picked up by international media and provoked a petition in the United States that was signed by leading feminists and women in the film industry.

What makes La Barbe unique is that it is an entirely decentralized organization, without any one leader or spokeswoman. A lot of the video footage from their protests is uploaded to YouTube in a very old-fashioned movie style, mimicking silent films from a bygone era, as if they are disrupting nineteenth- or early-twentieth-century worlds where male dominance was more accepted. Their message is often ironic, congratulating men on the system they have created and telling them how proud they are of them.

La Barbe activist Alice Coffin shared what happens during a demonstration: "At the beginning they are puzzled. They don't know if we are men or women. They get a little scared for a moment, as they feel they are losing control of the situation." Coffin told us that the responses really vary. "Sometimes the men are aggressive or make sexist comments or call you a clown. They call security and get you dragged out." Coffin was once locked in a closet after protesting at the Rugby Federation.

Being in La Barbe has given Coffin and many of her fellow activists more confidence. "It strengthens you," she told us. "You are no longer so afraid to say something." And the impact? "We have the power to make journalists react," Coffin said. "We get the media to report on important stories where there is a lack of gender diversity." Sometimes La Barbe has triggered internal conversations among the organizers of some of the events where they've intervened. "We get fan mail from people inside some of these institutions who thank us for saying something." Sometimes La Barbe is even invited by these institutions to give advice on gender inclusion. But Coffin told us that isn't their role. "We aren't experts or advisers. It isn't our business to come and advise you. We stick to being activists."

THE ACTIVIST GROUP THE YES MEN USES PROVOCATION IN A SIMILAR WAY. Built on a spirit of improvisation, Yes Men was created by fictitious personalities Jacques Servin and Igor Vamos (Andy Bichlbaum and Mike Bonanno, respectively), a pair of activists looking to expose the truth behind social, political, and economic issues.

We spoke with Andy Bichlbaum about the challenges of provocation. "It is hard to say what it is we are doing to shift things," he said. "In themselves, our actions don't really do anything, but in the context of a movement, they can do something." Like La Barbe, the Yes Men's primary lever for change is to grab media attention. "We provide excuses (often in the form of jokes) for journalists to cover important things."

Bichlbaum told us that the problem is there are all these "mainstream journalists who want to do something interesting and want to say something interesting, but they find themselves within these structures where they can't just cover something really important."

Pranking has always been part of Bichlbaum's DNA, but it wasn't until he was nearing thirty that he found a way to direct it to activism. His first activist prank was as a computer programmer at a gaming company. Bichlbaum was making a game called SimCopter and put kissing boys into the video game. "I did it out of annoyance at my job. I knew something would happen, but I didn't know what." When the game was released, it turned into a big media story, and Bichlbaum liked the attention. He wanted to keep doing corporate sabotage work, so he built a fake website where disgruntled employees could crowdfund ways to sabotage their companies.

A fake financing website for corporate sabotage was just the first step. Next, Bichlbaum and Bonanno built out the Yes Men as a public relations agency for "counter-cultural mischief activism." The Yes Men's first real success was a prank website that they set up in 2000 to amend the World Trade Organization's website on tariffs and trade (http://www.gatt.org/), adding: "At a Wharton Business School conference on business in Africa that took place on Saturday, November 11, the WTO announced the creation of a new, much-improved form of slavery for the parts of Africa that have been hardest hit by the 500-year history of free trade there."

As a result of this prank, Bichlbaum and Bonanno began receiving requests to represent the WTO in front of groups and organizations. They responded in the guise of official WTO representatives. The prank received international attention and gave the Yes Men a global platform.

Since the success of their WTO prank, they have continued to stage humorous, satirical hoaxes and share their improvisational practices through the Yes Lab, an incubator for activists. But Bichlbaum is careful not to overstate the impact of the Yes Men's pranks: "We grab media attention, but just talking doesn't change things. We can only help build pressure and interest."

What can you learn from provocateurs? Provocateurs like the Yes Men and La Barbe teach us not to compromise our vision or purpose. Provocateurs are also not afraid to challenge authority or fixed minds. Most of us can channel the spirit of provocation by becoming "myth busters in residence." We can shake up organizations in need of change by showing how certain ways of thinking are misguided or broken. But for many of us, our success as provocateurs comes with behaving gracefully and tactfully and knowing the right moments to ignite such conversations.

WHY CAN'T IT BE LIKE THIS ALL THE TIME?

One of the most historic cultures of provocation is that of the festival. In the summer of 2014, Tom Kenning decided to visit as many festivals as he could in England and mainland Europe to ask the question: "Why can't it be like this all the time?" Or: What can we learn from the festival spirit to inspire everyday life?

Historically, harvest festivals and religious festivals and feasts were used to usher in celebratory and sacred events that offered a departure from the hardship of everyday life. Many of today's festivals are big music festivals like Coachella and Glastonbury, but increasingly, there are more experimental festivals like the Secret Garden Party in England, the Borderland in Sweden, and Burning Man in Black Rock City, Nevada.

As Kenning told us, he was interested in exploring how the goodwill of festival culture could be brought "outside the festival gates to combat the tedium and isolation of working life." What he found was that for many, festivals provided an escape from self-consciousness. Festivalgoers were able to feel a sense of unity and connection. Festival life offered opportunities for spontaneity and the full experience of the senses. Not surprisingly, music, dance, and performance brought a greater embodiment than most found in the office. But aside from an increased appetite or fluency for talking to strangers and memories of freedom and flow, a lot of festival spirit seemed to vanish in the sobriety of normal life.

One group working to unlock festival spirit amid the humdrum of urban life is Morning Glory. Started in London in May 2013, Morning Glory offers sober morning raves for those who want to start their day with dance, smoothies, and wake-up massages. The raves start at six thirty A.M. and typically go until around ten thirty. While Morning Glory started as a provocation for the daily commuter to defy the typical morning routine, it has since grown to become a regular event operating worldwide.

After receiving hundreds of letters from people who wanted to bring the morning rave to their city, Morning Glory opted to franchise their model. They recruit "Glory Agents" or event producers around the world. Each Glory Agent is interviewed or given an "aura check," screened not only for their passion but also for their skills in event production, marketing, and public relations. Each agent is given a "Glory Guide," which is essentially a big manual outlining the principles, values, and business and branding guidelines of Morning Glory. In return for the Morning Glory affiliation, the franchisees pay a onetime licensing fee of around a thousand dollars and a small annual fee.

To date, Morning Glory operates in fourteen cities, including Barcelona, New York, London, Tokyo, Bangalore, and Melbourne. We asked New York producer Annie Fabricant why she thought Morning Glory was catching on and how it was impacting people. "It's funny to think of morning raves as life-changing, but they are. People leave buzzing and with a renewed faith in humanity. There is this explosion of energy and love that isn't dependent on alcohol or drugs. And that gives more meaning to people's lives."

While a lot of festival cultures may have dubious lasting impact, the ability to step into and imagine a world radically different from everyday life is the mandate of any provocation. The festival and the spaceship of science fiction are not so different—both offering temporary worlds that can help us to reimagine reality and fortify the operations of the imagination.

IN THE EARLY NINETIES, AT THE AGE OF SIXTEEN, TOM FARRAND AND HIS friends would frequent illegal raves across England. He remembers once driving a decked-out Ford Transit; on the road, one of his friends got an anonymous call. When they called the number, they were told to go to a gas station. At the gas station, they were directed to an empty field off a nearby highway. At that first rave, only three hundred people turned up. Around five years later, there were more than thirty thousand.

Raves weren't just a hedonistic outlet for Farrand. They were about creating a different kind of culture. "We had this collective experience," he told us. "A bucket went around if someone was running a generator, and everyone tossed in a bit of money. It was about feeling free, connecting to something bigger, and allowing for spontaneous organization."

As an adult, Farrand has spent over eighteen years working in brand and business innovation for companies including Procter & Gamble, WPP, and Oliver Wyman. In 2009 Farrand founded an organization called Good for Nothing that enabled him to merge his experiences with growing brands and managing innovation processes with those of attending raves.

Good for Nothing brings together innovators who want to "think, hack, and do" through "gigs," one-to-two-day pop-up events organized around a spirit of informality. "We let go of power and control and allow for people to self-organize and for ideas and collaborations to emerge naturally," Farrand told us.

Good for Nothing operates in more than twenty-five cities internationally, and some of the projects include tackling food waste, building out community infrastructure, and designing local campaigns to create energy-efficient homes. At one of the meetings, Good for Nothing called for all participants to show up at five P.M. at a random location in Suffolk, England. They were met by a 1930s bus and taken to a campground for the weekend to work on challenges that had been identified by the community. As at a rave, there was a feeling of immersion, of excitement, and of not knowing what would happen next.

HONORING THE TEMPORARY FICTION

The value of provoking is in starting a conversation. A protest movement doesn't last forever. A science fiction novel is only so many pages. A prank holds its surprise only so long before it is revealed. But groups of people who ask the right questions or probe alternatives often pave the way for true change to emerge. Cultures like live-action role-playing or Burning Man that pop up temporary worlds can generate insights that spill over into mainstream reality. We may not all want to spend all our time dressed in festival garb and bartering in a desert gift economy, isolated in a simulated Mars mission, or protesting in Zuccotti Park, but the temporary worlds created by the provocateurs spark dialogue in our mainstream culture and create the conditions for innovation to occur.

Chapter 6

PIVOT

FOR GIB BULLOCH, A CONSULTANT AT ACCENTURE, VOLUNTEERING WAS SOME-thing that other people did—until one day, while traveling on the London Underground, he saw an article in the *Financial Times* about volunteer opportunities for professionals abroad.

"I thought volunteer opportunities were only for doctors, nurses, and teachers, not businesspeople like me," Bulloch said. Intrigued, he applied and spent a year on a development project in the Balkans. Bulloch wasn't having a midlife crisis. He was happy in his role at Accenture; he was being challenged and thriving financially. Still, he wanted to explore an aspect that was missing in his day job: how business could make a more positive impact on the world.

Bulloch ended up in Macedonia for ten months. He traded

in the perks of being a management consultant (fancy hotels, business-class travel, and a comfortable salary) for a country destroyed by ethnic conflict and riddled with widespread poverty and unemployment. In an effort to improve the situation, he began to work in a business support center to develop the business skills and capacities of small- and medium-sized enterprises (SMEs). A little while into the experience, Bulloch realized how much more effective he could be if he had a team of consultants working with him. "There was a real lack of quality of business expertise among the people I met doing development in the Balkans," he told us.

In the depths of winter, and with "lots of time to think," he wondered: "Why is Accenture not here? Why are management consultancies not working in places like this?"

Bulloch felt he had stumbled upon a real market failure. "As a consultant, I was used to quality in terms of best practice, knowledge assets, and knowledge management. But working as a volunteer, I felt the development industry was pretty shabby and fragmented." Bulloch thought the development sector needed more professional skills.

As Bulloch prepared to leave the Balkans for a return flight back to London and his job at Accenture, he found himself at a little café in Thessaloniki, Greece, where he began drawing up a fake press release for a new business within Accenture. The article, Bulloch told us, described his vision of a consulting organization incubated within Accenture that would help professionalize development work.

The consulting practice built with Accenture resources and staff would focus on working with NGOs and donor organizations at "not for loss" rates: In other words it would create a nonprofit business within a for-profit business. Armed with a misfit idea, Bulloch needed to find a way to grab his superiors' attention. His faux article was just the hook. He wrote it as if it were issued by Accenture's chairman (bestowed with a fictitious knighthood in the text) at a future World Economic Forum in Davos, Switzerland. To quote the fake press release, which was boldly titled "Management Consultancy Giant Makes Far-Reaching Decree on the Role of Business in Society," the new consulting practice would aim to "maximize the global scale and business capabilities of the consulting giant, but focus on the greatest social need."

When he got back to London, Bulloch shared the press release with the head of Accenture in the UK, who had supported the company's volunteering efforts and had always been a champion of Bulloch's. This person forwarded the press release to the group's chairman, Sir Mark Moody-Stuart, whose interest was piqued, and he agreed to meet with Bulloch personally to discuss the idea over breakfast.

The morning of the breakfast, Bulloch woke up uncharacteristically late. "It was horrendous," he recalls. "This was the biggest meeting of my life, and I woke up thirty minutes before it was going to take place." He popped straight out of bed and into his suit without a shower. He made it just in time for the meeting, but this moment still haunts him: "If I hadn't woken up, my career would have taken a fundamentally different turn."

At the breakfast, the chairman asked some very pragmatic questions. Would people be willing to work for a lower salary? Was there a market in development, and would the development sector even want their services?

Bulloch was given the green light to do a bit more work to answer these questions. He put together a team of volunteers within the company to flesh out the business plan and ascertain whether there was a market for this sort of venture. "It was a very guerrilla approach to getting the idea off the ground," Bulloch told us. The team analyzed what the competition was doing and what the needs of the development sector were, and began refining the business model.

Bulloch then presented the team's findings to the industry heads within Accenture to secure the funding for a feasibility study. "One of the best pieces of advice that I got from one of the managing partners was that I needed to engage with the people in the firm who owned budgets: 'Go after the scary people,' he told me." Bulloch didn't want his initiative to be a dislocated part of the firm. It had to be embedded in the core business. So he began to court five people who controlled the budgets and could turn his vision into a key part of Accenture's business. Once he hooked three of those five, he could use them as leverage to pull the other two in. "There is definitely an art to being a misfit inside an organization," he said. "You need to know how to navigate the politics."

When all five were on board, Bulloch and his team sent out a survey to Accenture employees to ascertain whether they would opt to do development consulting and if they would do so on a reduced salary. They mapped the survey to the latest batch of performance ratings and found that the highest levels of interest within the company were among the high performers. "And that really was ammunition. We could tell the human resources unit: 'We need something like this.'"

In 2002 Bulloch started building the business. He took a salary reduction and built up an advisory committee of senior leaders within Accenture to oversee the fledgling unit. The first three pilot projects included a partnership with the Department for International Development (DFID), where Bulloch's team worked on improving the response of humanitarian information centers in Asia; a project in Vietnam with the nonprofit Care International for building the capacity of local staff; and an enterprise development in Serbia.

For Bulloch, this new practice was a way of keeping one foot in the corporate sector and one foot in the world that had inspired him during his work in the Balkans. That was exactly the type of hybrid leadership he was looking to catalyze at Accenture. "Can you blend a proposition to employees that offers the benefits of a traditional career with the opportunity to apply skills in a different way—where you have a feeling of purpose?" It seemed possible, but shaping this type of career path within a company focused on the bottom line was challenging.

"First you're selling this proposition externally to a development sector that doesn't necessarily see the problem—that has been weaned on pro bono consulting and handouts. Then you're selling this internally to a company that is accustomed to high margins and traditional corporate clients." At times, Bulloch admits, he was pushing in a completely different direction from the commercial interests of Accenture. But there was a significant value proposition to the company. Bulloch was bringing in new skills and capabilities.

Accenture employees received special training to work on development projects in Bulloch's division. He remembered, "The first pilot training we ran, we brought in this misfit guy with tattoos who was wearing jeans and a loose T-shirt who had worked in some pretty high-pressure situations in Nigeria and Cambodia. It differed dramatically from most of Accenture's trainings, where everyone is in a suit and tie and communicating in PowerPoint." In these training sessions, Bulloch worked to adapt the skills of Accenture's consultants by getting them to understand that, in many cases, they were there to listen and learn. They also had to learn about staying safe and being savvy on the ground.

Today Bulloch's consulting practice is called Accenture Development Partnerships (ADP). The division allows Accenture employees to rotate through the internal nonprofit—almost like a sabbatical—giving them the opportunity to work with clients in the development sector on projects ranging from reducing child malnutrition in Bangladesh to building sustainable solar energy in Uganda. The results are positive. The ADP team has worked in more than seventy countries and on more than two hundred projects a year. "We've delivered a quarter billion dollars' worth of services since starting," Bulloch explained. And yet, "People still ask me if this is my full-time job. It's insulting. Even with our track record, I still have to manage the corporate immune system of the firm. There are a lot of people and norms that want to snuff out things that are different."

On a personal level, Bulloch feels like a bit of a misfit. "We all feel alienated to a certain extent in the companies we work for. The boss of any organization can be quite a lonely role," he said empathetically. When Bulloch presents to NGOs, they often see him as "the guy from the evil private sector." And when he presents inside the business, he's "the wacky guy doing development work." Bulloch admitted: "I'm always the outsider."

Bulloch has learned a tremendous amount from this experience, particularly how to incubate start-ups within larger organizations. "Having a misfit idea is the easy part. The rest is finding air cover. You need protection from leadership. You need champions across the business." Bulloch explained that it can be very easy to suffocate innovation within large bureaucracies. "You can't apply the same management principles to a start-up that you use to manage a large corporation." For example, the policies and risk-management procedures that Accenture applies in large, mature commercial markets aren't applicable in a lot of the developing countries where ADP operates. While there are challenges and cultural mismatches between these start-ups and their corporate hosts, the former can help corporate DNA evolve. Bulloch told us that he is finding growing demand from the commercial for-profit businesses of Accenture for the skills and expertise ADP has around emerging markets, bottom-of-the-pyramid dynamics, and sustainability. "We are constantly being asked to be subject-matter experts on bids and proposals for commercial clients, because it can be quite differentiating."

It has been fifteen years since Bulloch returned from the Balkans. He is still working to get ADP into the bloodstream of Accenture. "Every day I'm challenging the idea that the only purpose of a company is to make money for its shareholders."

Reflecting on his journey, Bulloch offered, "You take one little step forward into the unknown, and it puts in motion this cascading process." He uses the metaphor of climbing a mountain: "As you climb higher and higher, you can see more and more around you, and how much further you have to go. When you're down in the valley, you try to get to a particular peak, and then you discover that peak is a foothill of a much bigger mountain."

By throwing himself into an uncomfortable and unknown situation where he dealt with issues that many believed to be outside the scope of business, Bulloch had an epiphany that he was able to bring back to his organization. His willingness to think existentially about the role of management consulting enabled him to create a whole new field around the hybrid career path. The experience that Bulloch had in the Balkans is now one that other Accenture consultants can share.

THE PERSONAL PIVOT

Innovation is traditionally defined by the things that happen *outside* of us: the hackneyed stories we tell of Ford manufacturing a car, Edison inventing the lightbulb, and Jobs creating the iPhone.

But what about internal innovation? Identity transformation? What innovative practices exist for navigating within ourselves? How do we find ways of connecting with what we want, what we need? And how do we build up the courage to pivot ourselves in a new direction?

It is quite common in business to talk about start-up pivots or strategic pivots related to organizations. But when we think about the meaning of "pivots" within the Misfit Economy, we are referencing *personal* pivots—the experience of enacting a dramatic change in the course of one's life to pursue greater fulfillment and inspiration, like Gib Bulloch did after volunteering in the Balkans.

Pivoting means having the courage to pursue a new path, even in the face of self-doubt, pressure from society, resistance within an organization, or community opposition. It entails a willingness to completely transform one's sense of self by stepping into the unknown, despite being uncertain. Like Alice's journey into Wonderland or Dorothy's trip down the yellow brick road, pivoting can mean heading out on an unknown adventure, not expecting a perfect destination.

PIVOTING A DEADLY STREET GANG

Growing up, Antonio Fernandez, like many Latinos, experienced racism. In third grade, his teacher called him a "spic," and in that moment he developed a hatred for "everything that was white, blue-eyed, and government." From then on, this little boy wanted to make sure that he would never again face that kind of disrespect. Later in that school year, the same teacher instructed him to "meditate—see yourself as you want to be, and it will come true." When he closed his eyes, his vision crystallized: He wanted to be a drug dealer.

By the time he was twenty-nine, Antonio Fernandez had surpassed his childhood expectations, inheriting the name King Tone and becoming the leader of the Almighty Latin King Nation (ALKN), the New York branch of the Latin Kings. The Latin Kings' own history is one of an organization founded on "misfit-ness." Originating in Chicago in the 1940s, the Latin Kings formed as a Puerto Rican social organization to tackle the prejudice of many of their white neighbors. With access to only migrant-level jobs and, later, factory work, the Latin Kings aimed to restore a sense of pride and identity to Latinos. From the get-go, these were individuals forced underground by a society that didn't recognize their talents, a society that treated them as subhuman.

While initially made up of Puerto Ricans, the Latin Kings

came to embody a larger Latino identity, attracting membership from Central and South America. But by the seventies, the Kings had lost their way, shedding the vestiges of the social organization they once were. In business-speak, we could say the Latin Kings experienced considerable "mission drift" as they pivoted to become a criminal organization and one of the largest drug-trafficking street gangs in the United States.

At the time when King Tone came to leadership, the Latin Kings were recovering from a deadly period of instability. The rapid growth of the ALKN had brought with it organizational chaos. Fernandez's predecessor, King Blood, had given an order for the murder of seven ALKN members who he felt had disobeyed him and threatened his rule. The most gruesome was the killing of William ("Lil Man") Cartegena, who was strangled, decapitated, and mutilated. For these actions, King Blood went to prison with a sentence of life in solitary confinement.

In assuming the leadership, Fernandez undertook a monumental pivot: His mission, as he saw it (departing from his childhood daydream of becoming a drug dealer), was to transform the Latin Kings from one of the reportedly "deadliest street gangs" in the country into an organization with a transformative civic agenda. It was a mission that, in Fernandez's mind, had precedent. "Gangs have been here since the beginning of New York. They split up this city—the Italians, the Irish, the Jews—and then they went on to become politicians, firemen, and lawyers." The difference between these ethnic groups and the Latin Kings was that the groups were allowed to evolve. "But as newer immigrants and as Latinos, we were not allowed the same growing pains."

FERNANDEZ WAS INITIATED INTO THE LATIN KINGS IN PRISON, AFTER BEING arrested multiple times while on parole, following an earlier arrest for dealing heroin. Arriving in prison at that time, Fernandez had felt deeply disappointed with himself. "All these things I thought I wanted [money and respect] hadn't brought me any fulfillment." But "after getting crowned [initiated into the Kings], I felt immediately different," he told us. "I felt that I was on a different path." He had spent his teenage years addicted to cocaine and running a successful drug-dealing business, but in the gang, Fernandez found the structure he believed he needed in his life to stay sober and disciplined. "After becoming a King, it solidified my belief that I was no longer going to be an addict. I had something else to live for."

It was in prison that the seeds for King Tone's pivot were sown. During his period of incarceration, Fernandez started gaining clarity around his purpose in life. "I knew I wasn't a bad person. I knew that even though I hurt people, I had a good moral fiber. I just didn't know what to do to become a better person, to achieve more in life. I didn't know where to go or what to do in order to attain the things I always wanted: to be respected, to be someone people could rely on and someone who could bring about change. I wanted to lead, just like I had led in the drug game. I wanted to use my natural talent for good."

It was this desire to bring about positive change within his community that inspired Tone's pivot. However, he knew it would be no easy task, changing a gang committed to criminal violence into an organization with a civic mission. Fernandez wanted the Kings to be perceived as a social movement, like the Black Panthers or the Nation of Islam.

For Fernandez, the transition was possible because the Kings had always maintained a kind of resistance identity. They just needed to reclaim and celebrate this aspect. Fernandez wanted to show that one of the deadliest street gangs was also human. Like many corporations, many gangs in the United States had become Goliath-style organizations. They were becoming undone by their size. The Latin Kings' unprecedented growth in the nineties brought internal divisions and strife. In corporations, these growing pains result in passive-aggressive emails, firings and redundancies, or frustrated phone calls; in a street organization, such instability is met by internal purging. Latin King members who were perceived as lacking loyalty were sentenced to execution by King Blood.

The organization had come to be governed by a military mentality that was once key to its survival but was no longer suited to the environment. The militancy of the New York chapter of the Latin Kings owed to their founding in the prison system where brutality was crucial to getting the organization off the ground. Outside of prison, however, members failed to adapt. As Fernandez told us, "The context had changed, but many of the members didn't have the skills for existing outside of prison. They weren't adapted for urban life, for employment, or for a peaceful coexistence in society." These misfits ran the risk of going through cycles of incarceration forever unless the Latin Kings could be changed.

Fernandez was working to put an end to the "gang-bang, shoot-'em-up" image, but converting gangsters into a powerful civil movement would require a groundswell of support from the Kings themselves. This would require Fernandez to build support from the ground up, using the different borough reps to be the ambassadors.

For Fernandez, humanizing an organization like the Kings brought a lot of resistance, both internally as well as from the outside world, where many didn't see the reforms as made in good faith. The FBI still labeled the Kings as societal deviants and threats to social harmony.

Within the Kings, there was resistance to becoming a more public-facing organization. Some gang members feared the Kings would lose the clandestine quality central to its organization, that Fernandez's efforts would bring the wrong kind of attention. "Identifying yourself is never good," he told us. "You're better off moving in the shadows."

But for the Latin Kings to realize Fernandez's vision of public servitude, they would have to be out there in the community. Gang members were directed to feed people, participate in a rally, or canvass for a politician.

Fernandez made sure not to drive the new strategy top-down. The genesis of his experiments in civic consciousness was the result of a secret society—a sort of internal task force—operating within the Kings during King Blood's rule.

When Fernandez took over, he sought to execute many of the task force's ideas. But it wasn't as simple as it seemed.

To ensure that local perspectives were considered, Fernandez visited each of the boroughs and went to local crown meetings, where he just listened. This listening allowed him to find out what people thought without relying on a hierarchy of communication. Fernandez made sure to prioritize many of the problems and needs of the different localities. As a result, when he began working with the different tribal ambassadors (those leaders of the different boroughs) to support the execution of the strategy, the response was positive.

To differentiate himself from the top-down, violent, and terrorizing leadership of his predecessor, Fernandez made sure not to tell people what to do but to hear out the perspectives of different boroughs. His ability to take in the opinions of the Latin Kings who weren't in high-up positions meant there was less resistance when the time came to make a switch in strategy. Everyone felt they knew the origin or source of Fernandez's thinking. For Fernandez, this strategy was partially self-motivated. In a gang, if you don't succeed in convincing everyone, someone might try to take you out. The Latin Kings had a culture of purging left over from King Blood's rule; it provided a powerful incentive for Fernandez to attempt to win over support. He didn't try to build total consensus, but he did make sure to hear each and every person.

As in nearly all change-management efforts, there were concerns about Fernandez's strategy. Some members of the Kings felt the organization should be split in two: that there should be a branch retaining militancy and another focusing on civic ideals. Fernandez was reluctant to split the Latin Kings. He was even approached by external political organizers who wanted to see him rebrand so they could fully politicize, cutting the strings to their gang origins. While Fernandez saw the case behind a rebranding, he felt the Latin Kings had built too much and come too far as an organization to consider spin-offs.

By keeping the Latin Kings intact, he felt he was helping the organization to evolve. Fernandez knew that if the organization maintained its militant approach, the Kings would become extinct by government crackdown. Like many CEOs, he worried that regulation would take the Kings out of the market altogether. He worked to inject a new spirit into the organization.

One of the concrete strategies that Fernandez saw as critical to the reeducation of the Latin Kings was to build external alliances around civic issues. The Kings worked with groups like Mothers Against Police Brutality to bring attention to the abuses of the New York City police force. They also worked with the Nation of Islam, Al Sharpton, and Jesse Jackson's Rainbow Coalition on an agenda of civil rights, social justice, and political activism.

Fernandez's aim was to attach the Kings to other organizations that were experienced in the ways he wanted the Kings to grow. By working with people like Richie Perez, a South Bronx teacher and social justice advocate, the Kings learned how to be part of nonviolent demonstrations. If the Kings wanted to become more involved in political rallies, they needed to learn the art of civil disobedience.

Many on the outside, notably the FBI, accused the Kings of being "a vicious gang with a PR campaign."[1] Many felt the Latin Kings' newfound civic consciousness was no more than a smoke screen for their criminal activities.

However, Fernandez's efforts were more than a public relations campaign. Within the organization, many of the gang members felt the change. One Latin King we spoke with remembered how the juveniles in the gang were kept separate from the adults. This strategy was new, a way of protecting young members from some of the militancy of the older Kings.

As we heard from one former Latin King (who wished to stay anonymous), "Fernandez didn't want us picking up any bad habits. They were trying to shield us from things." The young Latin Kings had to abide by curfews and needed their parents' permission to join the gang. They were also educated. Young Kings took regular classes on history and civil rights and were instructed in how to behave at rallies. In part, Fernandez realized that he couldn't win over or reeducate many of the older Kings accustomed to gangster life. But he could isolate the young and try to nurture different instincts among the next generation. There was hope that they could seek out legal employment opportunities. Fernandez went around speaking to businesses to encourage them to hire Latin Kings. He invited corporations to Latin King meetings, where they could witness firsthand the values of the organization and the sophisticated structure of management and order. As Fernandez told us,

"Everyone I knew was doing something illegal, but if I could get them a legal job, then they could make the transition."

Many of the Latin Kings, including Fernandez, never quite made it. Despite Fernandez's civic efforts, the legal economic opportunities weren't flowing fast enough, and the Kings continued their criminal activities, as the members depended on selling drugs for their livelihood. In June 1999 Fernandez was sentenced to twelve and a half years in prison for conspiring to deal cocaine and heroin. While he was never found in possession of these drugs, there was a video that placed him outside a building while a trade was going on. Many believed Fernandez was targeted because of his increasing political activity and the stand that the Latin Kings were taking against police brutality.

After being sent to prison, Fernandez spent three years in solitary confinement so that he wasn't allowed to communicate with any Latin Kings or get messages out to the gang. During this time alone, Fernandez told us how he spent "three hours in the morning and the evening just reminding myself of who I was and what my values were. I would pace the cell and just talk to myself." It was an intense, unpleasant period, during which he wrestled with his reasons for being there, his purpose.

After serving his sentence and getting out of prison, Fernandez had no choice but to rebuild his identity and his life. A condition of his release was that he was no longer allowed to call himself King or address the salutes of Latin Kings who would see him on the streets.

Since getting out of prison, he has gotten to spend time with his family and actively partake in the lives of his chil-

PIVOT

dren. Rather than going back to dealing drugs, today he applies his charismatic leadership in the fight to end violence in the streets. He now works in Newark, New Jersey, for a program that targets young people identified by the courts as "at risk," to help reduce the city's staggering crime and homicide rates. In 2013 the city of Newark saw the most violent twelve months it has experienced in over a quarter century, with more than a hundred violent deaths.[2] Fernandez's time in the streets made him an expert on violence and its drivers; his time in prison made him an expert on himself, his goals, and his values. In bridging these two worlds, he is now providing a valuable service to society.

"Youth only want three things," he told us, "love, belonging, and opportunity. If you take that away from them, they create it for themselves, and not always in the best way."

While Antonio Fernandez was ultimately unsuccessful in converting the Latin Kings into a legitimate civil organization, this does not detract from the scale of the transformation that he sought to bring about. Fernandez's personal pivot was triggered through exposure to civic leaders and the work of many New York–based activists. Often, as for Gib Bulloch, our personal pivots are triggered from a hunger to enter into the unknown or to build bridges between two seemingly different worlds.

BRINGING THE AMAZON TO NEW YORK CITY

Tyler Gage was a serious soccer player. By eighteen, he had been recruited to play soccer at Brown University and probably could have gone pro. But in his freshman year, he took a class called Religion Gone Wild, and things began to change. He felt a swell of interest in mythology and spiritual experience. "I felt trapped in this Western mind-set. I was a kid from the suburbs from a pretty secular household, and I wanted to know what else was out there," he told us.

On a whim, he reached out to an ethnobotanist who had done eighteen years of research in the Ecuadorian Amazon and asked if he could volunteer for the summer. A summer turned into two years, as Gage abandoned his pro-athlete aspirations and left behind his Ivy League school. After working with the ethnobotanist in Costa Rica, Gage went to Peru, where he spent nine months in the heart of the jungle with a tribe called the Shipibo. "I showed up with a tent and just threw myself into learning the language and customs of this tribe," Gage told us.

It was with the Shipibo that Gage started learning about indigenous spirituality and the tribe's respect for plants and nature. He took part in indigenous ceremonies and learned the songs that the villagers used to connect to the spirit world. "This is when a lot of my boundaries began to crack," Gage said. "Communicating with forces beyond what you could perceive was mind-blowing to me. The indigenous people I met had such a refined intuitive capacity."

With this experiment of living in the jungle, Gage began to feel that a lot of the things he used to care about were fading away. But he didn't have any spiritual epiphany per se. "It was just a process of learning how to be uncomfortable, of learning to be lost, and just being present with that."

After another year floating in and out of Peru and spending time in Brazil with some Amazonian religious groups, Gage plugged back into reality, returning reluctantly to Brown University. The summer before his senior year, he went back to Peru, but this time he heard chain saws cutting down hardwood trees. "The men cutting down the trees were the same ones telling me all these myths about taking care of the environment and the importance of nature," he said. Gage thought this was strange, but when he confronted the men, they told him it was a choice between cutting down trees or not having enough money to send their kids to school or get emergency medical care.

A bit disenchanted, Gage ended up taking a class on entrepreneurship during his last semester. In that course, he developed a business plan with friends around the concept of a beverage company that could employ Amazonian farmers. Their business plan was very well received and won some awards, but Gage graduated and thought of the business as a class project.

He received a Fulbright grant to study ethno-linguistics with the Shipibo. But Gage came to realize that just "hiding out and living with this tribe wouldn't really create impact in the world," he told us. "I just felt in my heart that I needed to start this company. It just felt right." He turned down the Fulbright grant and started doing research into creating a company based on the ideas he had sketched out in his earlier business plan.

Gage looked into the market for guayusa (pronounced "gwhy-you-sa"), an Amazonian "superleaf" that is brewed like tea and has as much caffeine as coffee and double the antioxidants of green tea. Despite its unique properties, guayusa had never been commercially produced in any capacity. Traditionally, it is drunk at three in the morning, when villagers convene around a fire, tell stories, and interpret dreams. To commercialize around guayusa, Gage had to learn about the plant. How do you harvest the leaves? How do you dry it? How do you export it? Are there import regulations?

Gage and his business partner, Daniel MacCombie, got money from the Ecuadorian government to figure out how to produce and export guayusa. They would have to build the entire supply chain from scratch, starting with the local producers. When they began talking to the indigenous communities in the Amazon about producing guayusa and selling it in bottled drinks in New York City, Gage said, they were not taken seriously. "These were communities that had been discriminated against for so long, so when these two young white guys came in telling them there were millions of people that would want to drink this product, they thought we were crazy."

But gradually, people started getting on board. Gage and MacCombie worked with village elders and local forestry engineers who had training and whom they could lean on to execute production in the jungle. They started exporting guayusa under the company name RUNA in 2010. For the first three years, Gage and MacCombie faced financial difficulty. Gage was so broke at one point that he realized he didn't have enough money to pay the ten-dollar airport exit tax to leave Ecuador. He had to go out and sell his headphones to a teenager in the airport parking lot. But they stuck with it, believing that if they just "spun the wheel, that things would happen."

Today RUNA is in seven thousand stores across the United States, purchasing almost one million pounds of fresh guayusa leaves from more than three thousand indigenous farming families in the Ecuadorian Amazon. The company spends over $350,000 a year purchasing the guayusa and invests an additional $50,000 a year in community development projects in the Amazon through a fair trade social premium fund. RUNA has also found success with consumers. The band Foo Fighters are fans of the drink, as is, Tyler Gage tells us, music executive Rick Rubin. And actor Channing Tatum is an investor and brand ambassador for the company.

If we zoom out, we see how one young man's experience of being a bit lost in the Amazon led to the creation of an incredible business. He was able to bridge his rabbit-hole experience with the real world. Today Gage splits his time between New York City and Ecuador to run the business. He told us that his "connection and commitment to indigenous spirituality has never been greater." At the same time, he can spend fifteen hours a day staring at Excel spreadsheets and doing logistics for his sales team.

With RUNA, Gage occupies two cultures. He often takes part in indigenous ceremonies and reconnects with the jungle, but he is also committed to running the company as a competitive business. His pivot is unique in that he found a way to leverage the resources and networks he had in the U.S. to support the world he came to know and love in the Amazon. This bridging of worlds is apparent in RUNA's advisers—a former executive, Tim Sullivan, who ran global logistics for PepsiCo and founded ZICO coconut water, as well as indigenous elders.

GETTING OFF THE GRID

As we've seen with Gib Bulloch's experience in Macedonia or Tyler Gage's adventure in the Amazon, time away can jump-start creativity and reflection because you are able to tune in to yourself at a deeper level. Increasingly, "hermit time" is sought by many young entrepreneurs who are finding inspiration by getting off the grid entirely, at least for short periods of time. "Digital detox" weekends and retreats, where people abandon technology and hold space for reflection, have become common. As Michel Bachmann, who runs a decelerator for entrepreneurs in Bali, told us, "It is about creating spaces to cut through the noise and refocus your energies on what really matters. We get so distracted and overwhelmed by the constant stream of information that we lose our sense of what's real."

Levi Felix, an entrepreneur in San Francisco, has benefited from this growing marketplace. Felix runs digital detoxes for entrepreneurs, as well as a summer camp for adults called Camp Grounded, in the California redwoods, where people leave behind their smartphones and unplug.

These offers are nothing new. The deceleration experience—getting away from society—is one that humans have toyed with for a long time. As theologian Henri Nouwen observed, "Solitude provides the furnace of transformation." It was in solitude on Walden Pond that misfit Henry Thoreau carried out his famous experiment in self-reliance and wrote, "If a man does not keep pace with his companions, perhaps it is because he hears a different drummer. Let him step to the music which he hears, however measured or far away."

More and more, the types of hermit instincts romanticized by Thoreau are beginning to seep into the entrepreneurial journey. That lifestyle isn't necessary or desirable for everybody, but removing yourself from obstacles and naysayers can be a gift in the development stage, when your vision is still forming. Solitude offers a space for incubating vision, for pivoting away from what you know or think you know. Sometimes, in escaping the pressures of society, the beeps and blips of technology, and forcibly removing ourselves from what we "do" every day, we can think and reconnect with a greater sense of purpose.

One entrepreneur we met with in San Francisco, Zach Verdin, did exactly that. Verdin and two of his cofounders lived on a remote island off the coast of Seattle. In exchange for taking care of one cat and thirteen chickens, the team was given shelter and a space to incubate their Internet venture. "We never talked about what we were doing as a start-up. We were on a mission to change the world and the Web for the better," Verdin told us. They ended up building a platform called New Hive, which offers a "blank canvas" for self-expression. The content on New Hive ranges from digital art books to gaudy GIFs, poetry, and personal confessions. Unlike other micro-publishing sites like Tumblr or Medium, New Hive gives its users a blank page to express whatever they want. Users are able to mash up text, audio, video, and images. The platform is still in its early phases, so its success is uncertain. But what the New Hive story points to is the power that spending time outside of society can have in catalyzing creativity and entrepreneurial vision.

"Being isolated gave us time and space to discuss our different ways of seeing the world, get a lot of work done undistracted, and meditate and brainstorm on long walks in nature," Verdin shared. Their start-up has a more existential quality due to their time off the grid. While some start-ups may be solely looking to cash in on the next social networking craze or build a myopic app, New Hive feels like it has a bit more soul. "We are trying to maintain a place on the Web where the Internet can be truly weird," Verdin told us.

THE ITCH TO ESCAPE ISN'T JUST FOR HERMIT WANNABES OR ASPIRING ENTRE-preneurs. Sometimes in leaving everything behind, you are forced to radically reinvent yourself.

FROM HARVARD M.D. TO ALIEN ABDUCTION EXPERT[3]

Dr. John E. Mack grew up in New York City in the 1930s and '40s. He attended Oberlin College and graduated with an M.D. from Harvard Medical School in 1955. As a trained psychoanalyst, Mack spent the early years of his career studying issues of childhood development and identity formation. He taught at Harvard for over thirty years, and in 1977 he won the Pulitzer Prize for his book on T. E. Lawrence, *A Prince of Our Disorder*. Mack was so well thought of in his field that in the eighties he was granted access to key political figures to better understand the root causes of the Cold War. Widely regarded as a skilled clinician, he cofounded the Cambridge Hospital Department of Psychiatry, a teaching hospital affiliated with Harvard University.

Throughout his career, and by virtue of his specialty, Mack was always interested in unusual people. However, in the late eighties, he became involved in research that jeopardized not only his career but also many of his friendships. He started studying alien abduction.

In first learning about the phenomenon of alien abduction, Mack was dubious; he recalled thinking that the people who reported alien encounters *had* to be crazy. Still, he began running hypnotic regressions from his home. The more time he spent with these patients, the more he realized they *weren't* mentally ill.

In 1994, Mack told an interviewer, "I think this is an authentic mystery, and I think we learn from saying, 'I don't know.'"[4]

This is one of the characteristics of the misfit pivot: You can't run from unknowns. Your curiosity forces you to embark on journeys where you don't have all the answers. True to misfit form, Mack dove in.

One of the research trips most convincing to Mack and his team was to a rural schoolhouse in Ruwa, Zimbabwe. At the Ariel School, sixty children between the ages of eight and twelve reportedly saw UFOs during a morning recess. The children recounted their experiences of seeing a spaceship and big black-eyed beings.

As Mack's former research assistant Dominique Callimanopulos told us, "I had been working with Mack on the abduction research, but I had always been a bit skeptical. But when I heard those children [from Zimbabwe], I knew their experiences were true. What they were describing, they weren't making up. I had young children of my own and knew when children lied, and these kids weren't lying."

Mack and his team ended up interviewing hundreds of people of various ages and backgrounds who claimed to have been abducted. Rather than label these experiences as a new disorder or syndrome, Mack argued that it was incumbent upon us, as a society, to alter our expectations and perceptions of reality to account for the phenomenon, a stand that drew much criticism.

"This doesn't belong in any discipline," Mack explained to

an interviewer in 1997. "It doesn't belong in mental health. It doesn't belong in physics. It doesn't belong in religion. It doesn't belong in anthropology. It doesn't belong in history of science. And yet each of these disciplines has something to contribute. The point is that if something doesn't fit our notions of reality, and yet the people who are having an experience that doesn't fit are of sound mind, are sincere, have nothing to gain, are in effect opening to other realities, then it seems to me the responsibility of academicians is to begin to question our notions of reality." [5]

Mack attributed society's failure to account for the abduction experience as a cultural shortcoming. Alien abductees weren't mentally ill or deranged, he posited—we just didn't have a way to interpret these experiences in our worldview.

Some of Mack's biggest critics called into question his use of hypnosis. In keeping with Freud's theory of repression—which held that the mind can banish traumatic memories to prevent us from experiencing anxiety—much of Mack's research invoked the idea of recovered memory, whereby, through hypnosis, a patient could go back into repressed trauma and recall additional details of their abduction experience, which prior to hypnosis may have been known to the patient only as a series of bizarre, confused fragments. The question was whether these repressed memories were mere artifacts of the mind or legitimate recollections. Mack's tendency toward a more literal interpretation of his patients' experiences with aliens was controversial.

Mack's transition into alien-abduction research was a profound pivot. As he went deeper into his studies, he came to realize that traditional science was limited in explaining many things about the cosmos. This conclusion brought him into direct conflict with his department, many of whom turned their backs on him, regarding his work as too "out there." Isolated from his family and in conflict with the academic establishment, Mack was able to turn to others for support. Among them were philanthropist Laurance Rockefeller, who helped fund his work; Woody Harrelson, who came to talk; and lawyer and Harvard legal professor Alan Dershowitz, who defended his right to academic freedom.

In 1994 the dean of Harvard Medical School brought together a committee of peers to investigate Mack's scholarship. It was, effectively, an inquisition, which left Mack feeling persecuted and misunderstood. While in the end the dean reaffirmed Dr. Mack's academic freedom in the face of the committee, the damage had been done.

In an interview that same year, Mack responded to critics, stating, "[A] criticism I face is that I'm a 'believer,' that this is a matter of faith and religion and not science and empiricism. I deeply question and challenge that. I arrived at my present understanding using every bit of clinical and psychological skill I had at my disposal in my forty years plus in the field, and then came to the conclusion that this phenomenon is in some way real. I did not make leaps of faith. This was not about beliefs. It was about the evolution of my thinking through my clinical work. Now did I use my whole psyche? My intuition? Yes. I think that's what a good mental health professional is supposed to do."[6]

As his professional credibility faltered, Mack's anxiety and anger rose. As Callimanopulos told us, "It was not easy for Mack to become persona non grata within the institutions he had helped to build." While always something of a misfit, Mack had coexisted productively within these mainstream systems. When the institutions called his integrity into question, Mack sought new allies. He grew his network and developed relationships with like-minded colleagues and friends. For anyone engaged in a profound pivot, keeping an entourage of supporters who really see you, can support you with transitions, and help you manage "naysayers" is essential.

You also have to learn to deal with the naysayers. Don't just be content with being the lonely, misunderstood outsider. If you switch directions, take people on the journey with you. Use language they will understand, and don't be frustrated if they don't get it right away. Be patient and know that any personal pivot involves ambiguity. And those unknowns can make us uncomfortable.

On a personal level, it wasn't always easy for Mack to hold these different worldviews within himself. He was uncertain how to commit himself fully to ideas that defied the training to which he had devoted his life's work. But the daring intellect that had distinguished his scientific career made it impossible for him to turn away from work that proffered such gripping questions of human identity and cosmic reality. Mack's deviation from the beliefs of his colleagues and his unconventional pursuit earned him the reputation of "that Harvard professor who believed in aliens." But his passionate inquiry gained him a community of support that was vital to his sanity and well-being.

Mack's story illustrates the potential hazards of the pivot. As romantic as it may seem, running off to fight windmills a la Don Quixote is not to be taken lightly. Indeed, the role of the misfit can be taxing. But John Mack wasn't afraid to ask big questions. History may judge him more favorably for his courage in publicly wrestling with the existence of aliens. But for many considering a pivot, Mack's story shows the enormous risk of straying too far. As Mack went further and further into the consciousness of experiencers, he became ever more isolated from the Harvard world and scientific establishment.

For many misfits, the process of innovation may not be glamorous. Instant gratification and acceptance of your ideas are rare. Sometimes we can travel too far into the future, finding ourselves far afield of what reality can accept.

Many of the misfits in this chapter who embarked on extraordinary personal pivots courted controversy or were misunderstood, as in the case of Dr. John Mack or Antonio Fernandez. In other instances, as with the story of Gib Bulloch, the pivot away from mainstream success meant that these misfits must still prove themselves, locked in a struggle to get society (or a company) to see and value them.

Regardless, these stories show how unwavering belief,

commitment to core values, and an unwillingness to let the opinions of others dictate their existence can help individuals undertake a personal pivot that moves their life in a new and ultimately more personally fulfilling direction, even if it is not always fully understood.

Part 3

THE MISFIT REVOLUTION

Chapter 7

WALKING THE MISFIT PATH

JASON CLAY GREW UP ON A SMALL FARM IN KING CITY, MISSOURI. AT THE AGE of four, he was already planting potatoes and driving a tractor. With six brothers and sisters, Clay knew what it was like to grow up poor. But the pressure increased when he was fifteen and his father was killed in a tractor accident. This left Clay to manage the family farm with his mother while putting himself through high school and participating in varsity athletics— football, basketball, and track.

Today Clay is a senior vice president at World Wildlife Fund (WWF), leading work on global agricultural stewardship. He has also played a role in the genesis of this book in a biological sense, as he is Alexa Clay's father. Growing up, Alexa witnessed firsthand the life of a misfit.

This past year, after nearly a decade of work, Jason Clay succeeded in getting fifteen companies—representing nearly 70 percent of global salmon production—to commit to sourcing their salmon sustainably by 2020. Clay regularly meets with CEOs of major companies to help them understand how global issues and trends will affect their companies. His journey, however, from small-town farmer and football quarterback to a position where he has increasing influence over how we live on a finite planet has not always been easy.

Clay believes his background in farming shaped the way he thinks. "As a farmer, you learn that perfect is the enemy of good. Good enough is fine. Farmers have to solve problems in a resourceful way." Growing up with little to no money, he learned how to act frugally, a mind-set that he leverages in his work today. "You can solve problems without just throwing money at them. It's often less about what to think and more about how to think."

In working with Coca-Cola, for example, Clay challenged the company to think about their water consumption differently. He urged them not to focus on water consumption at the bottling plant level but at the sugar production level, as water consumption at the sugar production level can be fifty times more intensive than at the bottling plant level. What Clay has tried to get companies to realize is that many of their biggest environmental impacts happen outside of their control. So an important strategy for these companies is to work with their supply chains.

At the age of eighteen, Clay—after being the first person in his town to take the SATs—earned a scholarship to attend Harvard University. He immediately felt like an outsider. "I didn't meet another farmer there," he said. "But it wasn't just that I was poor, it was that I didn't share any experiences with people. I wasn't a skier, didn't go on holiday in Europe during the summer." While he had amassed great life experiences, his journey didn't connect with that of his peers. Academically, Clay faced another steep learning curve: He had written only one paper in high school. Life in a small town was more about an oral tradition. After reading his first paper, his freshman writing instructor asked if English was his first language.

Clay found himself drawn to anthropology in part because, for him, life at Harvard was like stumbling into a lost Amazonian tribe. He had to learn the customs—how to think before he spoke, how to eat correctly, and which utensils to use. He also learned how to be frugal in the face of affluence. It took him two months to pay off one early phone bill, for example.

In anthropology, he found that his outsider identity could be useful—that observing cultures and how they operated was an important part of understanding the world. He also learned (to his surprise) that he could make more money using his head than his hands. He ended up doing a Ph.D. in anthropology at Cornell University, focusing his research on smallholder farmers in Brazil. "In many ways, I identified more with those farmers than I ever did with my peers at Harvard. I knew their world, what their concerns were, and what questions to ask.

We had a common background—we planted, cared for, and harvested crops. We all knew how fickle the weather is, for example."

Upon his return from Brazil, Clay tried his hand teaching at Harvard and then working for the U.S. Agency for International Development, but he felt suffocated at both. Neither option let him keep learning. So he decided to volunteer for Cultural Survival, a human rights group that worked with indigenous people globally. After becoming a specialist in predicting human rights violations and the number of body bags needed in refugee and famine camps, Clay happened to meet Ben Cohen, of Ben & Jerry's, after a Grateful Dead benefit for the rain forest. Together they came up with an idea to help support people living sustainably within rain forests: a new ice cream flavor (Rainforest Crunch) from which Ben & Jerry's would donate a share of the sales to rain forest inhabitants in Brazil. Generating income for indigenous people not only proved the value of the rain forest, it also generated income so that members of indigenous communities could hire lawyers to defend their own land rights against encroaching companies.

This experience led Clay to become a pioneer of rain forest marketing. In 1989 he started a nonprofit trading arm of Cultural Survival, which purchased fruits, nuts, oils, honey, pigments, and spices from indigenous communities in the Amazon. Within four years, they had tripled the price they were paying Brazil nut harvesters, and the rest of the industry responded by doubling their price. It was a similar model to the one Tyler Gage started with RUNA, but Clay was advocating the idea back in the 1980s, before anyone had heard about fair trade or certification. Clay formed partnerships with brands like Ben & Jerry's, the Body Shop, Odwalla, and Stonyfield, but he faced a lot of backlash from folks who were more interested in preserving indigenous culture than generating livelihoods for those communities.

Ultimately, Clay was perceived as undermining Cultural Survival's mandate of documenting the plight of indigenous people by creating too much of a business. The trading company within the NGO required millions of dollars of working capital, and the Harvard-based board was not comfortable overseeing such a venture, so he was fired. He had pushed his employers too far outside their comfort zone. Moreover, his work was getting a lot of attention, and the founder of Cultural Survival came to see him as a threat. Clay remembers crying out of frustration. But he recognized the challenge of doing something that no one had ever done. The conflict helped him to develop a thicker skin. He withdrew, regenerated, and sought out the comfort of his spouse, close friends, and allies who believed in him and the change he was trying to bring to the world.

Today Clay's thinking is resonating. "Connecting local producers with international markets has become a go-to strategy for livelihood generation. It is no longer controversial," Clay told us. After decades of hard work, Clay has found an audience. He is a regular TED speaker, and he is working with leading corporate CEOs from Unilever, Mars, General Mills, Nutreco, Rabobank, McDonald's, Cargill, and even the

World Bank on sustainable agriculture. His approach has also changed. He has learned how to operate as a misfit within the system.

Clay is now more committed to meeting people where they are, rather than forcing his view upon them or being frustrated with them for not accepting his perspective. "You need to listen twice as much as you talk, because as long as people are preoccupied with their own problems, they are never going to see the bigger issues."

This is something that we found in talking with a lot of misfits working within big organizations, such as David Berdish at Ford or Gib Bulloch at Accenture. It's important to understand the politics and motivations of the people you work with and the people you are trying to influence. Many people operate from a position of fear—fear of failure, fear of reputation, fear of the unknown. And so you need to be able to stop and ask yourself: What motivates a person at a deeper level? How can I better understand his or her point of view? Don't forget to turn that mirror on yourself and understand the biases and fears that you bring to a situation.

Being a misfit requires that you have a bit of double consciousness: able to see the logic and rationality of others' viewpoints while maintaining your own conviction. It also requires a long-term perspective. The hack, provocation, or hustle that you are trying to bring to the world might take some time to find acceptance. This is something that Clay knows all too well. "There is no scarcity of ideas. Sometimes they die. Sometimes I resurrect them ten to twenty years later and dust them off when the climate is more receptive or when I know how to make a better pitch."

Over time, Clay came to appreciate the instincts of the copycat. He recognized that he could generate far more ideas than he could ever take to scale, so he began to share all of his ideas rather than holding on to them. For him, ideas were like seeds and brains like soil: Sometimes the seeds took root, other times they perished, and in some instances they lay dormant for years before sprouting.

Part of what grounds Clay during the ups and downs of the misfit journey, he credits to his farming roots. "I learned to create my own opportunities but to also let go when things don't work," he said. "I didn't let money drive my life, and I stayed focused on the results I wanted." He told us that as a farmer, you realize failure is inevitable. Sometimes failure can be due to your own efforts, but more often it is because of something outside of your control. You can have a bad season: too much or too little rain, for example. Clay said that he learned to rebound after disappointments and try again. He kept many balls in the air, not investing too much energy in one project or initiative. This kind of diversification was something he learned in farming. At the age of four, he was already learning about spreading risk by planting different crops that thrived under varying conditions.

TRANSFORMING THE CULTURES AROUND YOU

What misfits like Jason Clay or Chas Bountra, who is building our collective capacity for R&D in the pharmaceutical sector, or our bearded-feminist pranksters La Barbe have in common is they aren't lone innovators working in a vacuum to grow the success of their ideas; they are working to transform the cultures around them.

As we think about how to apply the skills of hustling, hacking, copying, provoking, and pivoting in our lives and work, we're ultimately faced with a much bigger challenge than harnessing a behavior or mind-set. We are faced with the enormity of changing the systems and norms around us. And that can be a much slower process.

Mandar Apte, a chemical engineer, is seeking to transform the culture of Shell. Apte spent over a decade earning his credibility and building relationships, while doing technical roles in oil and gas production, technology, and strategy, before he had a novel idea to use a meditation-based learning program to empower colleagues and nourish the innovation culture at Shell. To truly infect the culture of the company, he initially worked with the company's secretaries to pilot a one-hour taster workshop. Pretty soon these workshops were being organized from the bottom up across various departments. From there he was able to build enough momentum to get management support to design and deliver the program. At the time of writing, more than two thousand Shell staff members have participated in the meditation-based learning modules from across the company's offices in the UK, Brazil, the U.S., the Netherlands, Malaysia, India, Singapore, and the UAE.

Apte is also testing the benefit of yogic breathing and meditation techniques to enhance the safety culture at Shell, which is of critical importance in the oil and gas industry. As part of the investigation, drivers of Shell's trucks in India and workers at a refinery in Louisiana are participating in the pilot program. If the results of this experiment are positive, they would enable greater workplace safety in many industries where focus and attention on task is key to success—for example, mining and construction or medical surgery.

Other types of "culture hacks" can be simpler acts of insurgency. Heidi McDonald, a video game designer, decorates her desk at work with a pirate ship and is planning to get a skull and crossbones tattoo. David Berdish, who was looking to reinvent mobility at Ford, was very open at work about his Catholic faith. Sometimes the simplest change we can make to a culture is to bring our passions and values to work.

For McDonald, pirates "stand for independence and adventure. You have the freedom to make your own rules, and your life depends on your own resourcefulness," she told us. She brings these pirate values to her work. But as she said, "I don't have to be concerned about waving my freak flag; the whole industry of gaming is run by geeks and misfits."

Working in a more traditional industry, Berdish credits a lot of his success in developing human rights practices for

Ford to his spirituality. A few others on his team were open about their faith. As he told us, "We had a commitment to human rights because of our faith." For Berdish, spirituality is something that can and should be more visible at the workplace. "Checking your spirituality at the door is similar to checking your being at the door. You need to bring your soul to work."

The success of Apte's meditation program also owed to his bringing authenticity and values into the workplace. An active practitioner and trainer of meditation, Apte found it natural to share the ancient practice in the workplace. It may seem obvious, but in allowing ourselves to bring our values into our work, we help to shape the cultures we are a part of rather than conforming to them. A significant majority of the misfits we spoke with (aside from the con artists, of course) had this commitment to authenticity in common.

As jazz musician Harold O'Neal told us, "I feel that everyone is unique. If we are all ourselves, then we are all misfits. I do my best to stay connected to what's going on inside of me to keep in tune with my uniqueness." Being able to turn inward and listen deeply to yourself in the way O'Neal describes is liberating, but it is also a leap if you aren't used to doing it. You need to give yourself the permission to cast aside the roles and guises. You have to find the courage to dig beneath all those layers that society thrusts upon us and try to rediscover those true callings. You need to become okay with no longer blindly aligning with the pack. And walking that path of the black sheep over the course of a lifetime can be challenging.

THE UPS AND DOWNS OF MISFIT RESILIENCE

After leaving his prestigious job at San Francisco General Hospital, Dr. Gary Slutkin spent ten years working to stop the spread of infectious disease in Africa. After a decade, he was burnt out from witnessing so much death and disease. "Epidemic death has a different feel to it—it is full of not only fear but panic. I had repeatedly heard hundreds and thousands of women wailing and crying in the desert," he told us.

After working so hard in such trying circumstances, Slutkin just wanted to go back home and start over. "I was feeling physically exhausted, chronically jet-lagged, and emotionally isolated," he told us. His work with Cure Violence also takes a huge amount of energy and perseverance. "Getting the system to completely rethink its approach to violence comes with a lot of pushback."

To keep himself sane, Slutkin has found better ways of managing his energy. "I'm very sensitive to the way I feel—in particular, to whether there is this feeling of being on overload. If I'm talking too much, thinking too much, I feel like I'm on overload, and that's the time to take a walk or slow things down." Slutkin creates blank space for himself. He often puts holes in his schedule where he isn't allowed to do anything. In this time, "the brain gets a chance to process all that has happened. It isn't just meditation and mindfulness but stopping the input. Stop reading, stop talking, and stop looking at media."

Catherine Hoke, the misfit who started Defy Ventures to connect ex-prisoners with entrepreneurial opportunities, has also been incredibly challenged by her work. With the Prison Entrepreneurship Program, which she started before Defy, she drove herself to points of exhaustion. She was so focused on the success of the program that her first marriage dissolved and she was left feeling desperate and alone. "PEP was growing so fast, and I was eating at gas stations because I had no time. My health was deteriorating, and I was falling apart because of the stress."

Some of Hoke's ex-students ended up taking care of her during her divorce. "These guys out of prison were the ones I felt comfortable being real and fragile around." In a very needy state, Hoke ended up having inappropriate relationships with some of these ex-students and resigning from her position, which brought a whole other wave of darkness where she really questioned whether life was worth living. Hoke admits that she was afraid of showing weakness and of being judged or shunned for her actions. "I hated myself and my life. I had lost my identity [as a wife], I had lost my profession [at PEP], and I had no money."

Following a public resignation and admission of the inappropriate relationships, Hoke received a thousand letters of love and support from people who stuck by her. She credits her circle of friends and supporters—as well as her faith—as critical to her rebound. "I left Texas and PEP with nothing. It was like a sad country song. I had invested my entire life savings in the program. I got to New York, and friends put me up, and I slowly started to rebuild."

In New York, Hoke went through intensive therapy, grew spiritually, and read a lot about grace, love, and redemption; she sought out stories of others who bounced back. But Hoke cautions other misfits: "Figure out if this is the right thing to give yourself to. If you don't have the greatest level of conviction in the dream and the vision—if you don't believe it with every bone in your body—then it's not worth it." For Hoke, there is never a Plan B. She gives everything she has to Defy Ventures. "It's a hard path. Because you are selling your vision all the time to so many people who don't see the world as you do."

A piece of advice that Hoke offers to misfits learning to manage their resilience is to get used to the word no. "Don't let no kill you," she says. Officials in one of the first prisons where Hoke attempted to start an entrepreneurship program told her the idea was too crazy. They threw her out of the prison and wouldn't let her work there. She remembers crying for three hours. Today, however, Hoke has become accustomed to hearing the word no. She still doesn't like it, but she doesn't take it personally. "I am willing to take unlimited criticism. If I get criticism, I double-check it with other people that I trust. And not just yes people, but people who will push me and be honest if I'm not on the right path."

Tyler Gage, the young misfit who spent time in the jungle before starting his business selling tea from the Amazon, is another for whom there is no Plan B. "I am completely surrendered to RUNA [his business]. I think a big reason we have been successful is because we haven't slept. We've just hustled. There aren't a ton of substitutes for hard work and just the grit to get stuff down." Gage is still under thirty, and this is his first venture. But as much as he functions without sleep and with an overdependence on caffeine (he confesses), he also spends a few months of the year in the jungle, where he can detox a bit from Excel spreadsheets and the hustle of sales.

Before committing to something that could consume your whole life, you have to ask yourself: "Is this mine to do?" Gage, Hoke, and Slutkin couldn't imagine doing anything else. The sacrifice and sweat they put into their work is what brings meaning and purpose to their lives. As exhausting as the work can be, it also provides them with energy and deep fulfillment. The challenge for them is remembering that they don't always have to be sprinting. Sometimes you need to approach your work like a marathon, not giving up all your energy in the first few miles.

At the same time, the pace of life can be very uneven. As Clay told us, "There are critical points where you have to act immediately and where there is no time to lose. Life gives you limited chances; you need to take advantage of them."

Compared to some of our other protagonists, Clay sees himself as a serial misfit; he has moved between very different networks: academia, human rights, environment, and the private sector. He is also the first to acknowledge that the journey would have been impossible if not for a spouse who not only understood his journey but also shared his sense of purpose. For him, it is a journey best not taken alone.

THE POWER OF THE ENTOURAGE

In the modern world, misfits don't have guilds to foster their skills and development. They have entourages. For the gangster surrounded by his "associates," the pirate captain dwelling amid a ship full of "mates," or the politically motivated hacker who finds like-minded revolutionaries in the cyber-world, having an entourage not only strengthens personal resilience, it also helps ideas reach new heights.

In its simplest form, an entourage provides an incubator for cultivating your inner misfit. Through an entourage, you can discover a network of trust that liberates you from the pressure to conform. A misfit alone is a recluse, alienated and cut off from the world. A misfit with a tight community can be far more influential.

In 1921 the young aspiring American writer Ernest Hemingway moved to Paris, where he faced poverty, drank himself senseless, fell deeply in and out of love, and, having found his voice as a writer, became a true innovator of the written word. But Hemingway's transformation isn't a story of lone genius; like many an innovator, he owed a substantial debt to a collective, notably the expatriates who gathered in Paris in the 1920s.

Beyond the myth of rugged individualism surrounding him, Hemingway benefited from the commitment, mentoring, and support of this small group of people—an entourage, if you will. While our modern culture tends to associate the word with celebrities and motorcades, the pure definition is more commonplace, referring not to the rank or importance of the person at the center of the circle but instead to "one's associates" or (from the Old French *entour*) "one's surroundings." If he hadn't had the support of those around him, the world might never have witnessed the writer we know to be Hemingway.

The members of Hemingway's entourage were varied but bonded in their common support. Sherwood Anderson, a Chicago-based writer, was one of the first to recognize Hemingway's talent and introduce him to publishers. Anderson also enticed Hemingway with the idea of going to Paris and provided him with letters of introduction.

Then there was Sylvia Beach of Shakespeare and Company. What would have become of him were it not for Sylvia Beach? Beach loaned Hemingway money when he was hungry for food and books when he was hungry for inspiration. There was Ezra Pound, whom Hemingway praised for his kindness. "Ezra was one of the most generous writers I have ever known," he wrote in *A Moveable Feast*. "He helped poets, painters, sculptors, and prose writers that he believed in, and he would help anyone whether he believed in them or not if they were in trouble."

In *The Paris Years*, Michael Reynolds perfectly captures the spirit of Hemingway's bohemian entourage: a community of writers and artists a stone's throw away from one another, energized by their proximity, their collective enthusiasm, and their common ambition:

Less than two blocks from Hemingway's table, what was left of Charles Baudelaire and Guy de Maupassant lay beneath stone memorials in the Montparnasse cemetery. A five-minute walk down Boulevard Raspail, Gertrude Stein and Alice Toklas were planning their Christmas meal. Close by Ezra Pound was reading through a bit of manuscript left him by a young friend with exhausted nerves, Tom Eliot, on his way to a rest cure in Lausanne. Eventually Eliot would call it "The Waste Land." Less than two blocks from the Hemingways' hotel, James Joyce was dressing to attend a party at Sylvia Beach's bookstore, Shakespeare and Company, where he would celebrate the final revisions to his manuscript *Ulysses*.

Then there was Gertrude Stein. Apart from offering Hemingway feedback on his early drafts, Stein played a big part in connecting these like-minded misfits. Every Saturday evening, Stein hosted a salon in her flat on 27 Rue de Fleurus in Paris. Attendees included Picasso, Fitzgerald, Joyce, Matisse, and Hemingway, among others. In providing a refuge for conversation and inspiration, and in supporting and nurturing talent, Stein began an experiment that today's artists, writers, designers, and entrepreneurs strive to re-create. The perfect writers' group, artists' collective, entrepreneurial incubator, rapper crew, co-workspace, and hacker collective is an imitation of Stein's salon. All are seeking transformation through connection; all are striving to transcend the isolation that can accompany the creative process. The truth of the entourage is that we make our mark on the world not only as individuals but also by helping others.

CULTURES OF INFORMALITY

If there is anything that misfits need most (aside from an entourage), it is an environment that offers flexibility. What Gib Bulloch sought from Accenture was an environment receptive to his ideas—a corporate culture where he could reinvent his job description. What provocateurs like Yes Men, La Barbe, and the UX thrive on is a spirit of improvisation to operate outside of traditional systems. Historic pirates could come up with new systems of governance aboard their own vessels. Misfits need space to live by their own rules.

That means if we want to tap the power of misfits, then our formal institutions have to start becoming better hosts. Popular exposure to festivals like Burning Man, movements like Occupy, hacker collectives, and co-working spaces built around egalitarian principles mean that workplace expectations are changing. At the sight of command and control systems, misfits bolt.

One of the interesting side effects from the Occupy movement observed by journalist Nathan Schneider: "When people from Occupy went back to work they realized how their workplaces were run on so little democracy. Occupy gave people a glimpse into a different way of being part of an organization—one where participation and self-determination were everything."

This discontent is something that business thinker and author Dov Seidman has observed, too:

> Like most protest movements, Occupy Wall Street demonstrators are demanding freedom from the current system. Many employees want freedom from command and control bosses and task-based jobs and freedom to contribute their character, creativity and collaborative spirit at work in pursuit of a values-based mission worthy of their dedication.[1]

With many employees jaded by command and control systems, some organizations have sought to abolish hierarchies and function with greater informality. The Seattle-based Valve is a billion-dollar gaming company (responsible for games such as Half-Life and Portal and the software distribution platform Steam) that runs without any corporate hierarchy. In lieu of traditional authority, Valve employees have to be incredibly self-motivated. Every employee is accountable for the organization's success or failure. Employees are encouraged to work together in self-organized "cliques of labor."

Salaries are based on reputational currency. Valve employees working on the same project rank each other's ability to collaborate, technical skills, and overall performance. These rankings are used to create a company leader board that determines how much each employee gets paid.

Semco, a leading manufacturer and one of Brazil's fastest-growing companies, is experimenting with a similar approach by allowing employees to set their own hours, salaries, and even bonuses.

Certainly, social movements or activist collectives like Occupy and La Barbe allow individuals to function in different kinds of cultures with more decentralization and collective ownership. The question is to what extent these subcultures will influence mainstream workplaces. So far, we've seen that in experiencing these alternative cultures and exploring more relaxed hierarchies, many are coming to question the command-and-control systems we are born into.

Remember Angelo Vermeulen, who commanded the simulated Mars mission? He experimented with very different models of leadership, giving away his commander role, allowing different crew members to lead for periods of time, and asking them to evaluate that experience. Vermeulen told us that he learned a lot about his own leadership during the mission. "A leader is always modifying a situation in their interests in order to lead. As a leader, I have these needs in order to be able to lead. Social interaction is one of my main needs—and so part of my leadership is to maximize social interaction because it's part of my value system."

Vermeulen questions the popular idea that equates a lot of starship and space exploration culture with military culture. In a typical mission, ground control dictates the astronaut's experience. The astronaut is essentially an operator. But Vermeulen is interested in more horizontal and participatory cultures. "There will come a moment when ground control can no longer control every minute of space inhabitants' lives,"

Vermeulen told us. As Valve and Semco are exploring more self-governing cultures of organization, Vermeulen thinks the same participatory cultures can live aboard starships and govern future space colonies. But how do we bring some of these experimental cultures down to earth?

CONCLUSION

ZOOM INTO A FUTURE WORLD WHERE THE "MISFIT REVOLUTION" HAS OC-
curred. What does it look like? How do you get there? The
world we imagine is one where conventions are constantly
questioned; where innovators who possess different hacks are
not only accepted but also celebrated. A business is no longer
just about conforming to a job description but about unlocking the entrepreneurial and positive deviance of employees. Innovation is no longer just about the newest gadget but about
addressing our deepest needs as a global community. Criminals
are no longer burdens to society; their expertise is not locked
away but valued and repurposed for society's benefit. Students
no longer work to fit themselves into educational environments to "consume" knowledge, but direct their own studies

to develop their passions and knowledge in collaboration with others.

Let us be clear: It's not a utopia. It's a world that is slowly being revealed. More and more, misfit ideas are beginning to spill over into mainstream culture. In the corporate world, Maggie de Pree is someone who is trying to foster new misfit ecosystems at large companies. De Pree cofounded (with Alexa, coauthor of this book) a network called the League of Intrapreneurs, bringing together entrepreneurial misfits from across Fortune 500 companies. The remit of the league is to build entrepreneurial capacity inside large companies by supporting misfit ideas that generate value for both business and society. Imagine a world where corporate ecosystems behave a bit more like venture ecosystems, tapping the full talents of their employees; where hierarchies can be overstepped in the service of good ideas.

In the field of education, a group of emerging thinkers called Wisdom Hackers has come together to see how to build up a community for peer-to-peer philosophy. The aim is to build an informal collective, much like the structure of Anonymous or a loose guild or entourage, to enable individuals to carve out space to wrestle with big questions. Wisdom Hackers occurs outside of traditional educational environments and provides tools for any community to "download" and initiate an inquiry into life's "burning questions."

Misfit ideas are also beginning to mainstream in housing. Hippie notions of cooperatives and "intentional community" are being refreshed for modern lifestyles. In San Francisco, the Embassy Network is a network of shared living spaces that busy creative professionals or travelers can plug into. Berlin cooperative housing units such as Lighthouse and Hain 24 allow autonomy through private apartments but have common areas and resources for a diverse group of residents, including singles, families, and retirees.

Are there other signs of misfit revolt? Morning raves are transforming the commute of the urban professional in London, New York, Barcelona, and Tokyo. In Paris, the biohacker-space known as La Paillasse offers a community-based public laboratory for citizens to try their hand at biology and bio-technology. And the growing number of those freelancing is making hustlers and entrepreneurs out of a new creative class.

While some misfit markets or approaches are still nascent and struggling to gain popular appeal (for example, camel milk, a belief in aliens, a pipeline between prisons and the world of venture capital), little by little, as we all start "coming out" as misfits, a world is emerging that accepts and nurtures the un-conventional.

ACKNOWLEDGMENTS

THIS BOOK OWES ITS EXISTENCE TO AN INCREDIBLE ENTOURAGE OF MISFITS around the world who served up their life stories and offered us support and guidance. Without you, this book never would have materialized. Thank you. Thank you to our incredible agent, Christy Fletcher of Fletcher & Co., who was a continuous source of strength and pragmatic advice. To our editor, Ben Loehnen, who kept us to high quality standards and made this book immeasurably better. To Laureen Rowland, who helped us get early drafts into something coherent and turned two first-time authors into more confident writers. And to Emily Loose, who believed in this book from the get-go and encouraged us to continue in our endeavor to write it.

Thanks to our friends and colleagues who recognize and

champion the importance of the informal and makeshift economies, including Steve Daniels, Robert Neuwirth, Simone Ahuja, Navi Radjou, Garance Choko, Lee-Sean Huang, and Adam White. To Peter Sims for opening doors for society's "black sheep" and connecting us with his publisher. To Maggie de Pree for helping us dive into the world of corporate misfits. And to Lance Weiler and Tim Leberecht for being sources of inspiration and connection.

Our time on the ground in India would have been a disaster had it not been for the support and guidance of Jairaj Mashru. Thank you for your commitment and your belief in this project. And thanks to Hussain for showing us a glimpse of the underground world in Bombay.

In New York, we have to thank Catherine Hoke, who invited us to meet the incredible ex-gangsters and former drug dealers who are "transforming their hustle" as part of Defy Ventures. To Antonio Fernandez, who shared his inspired story of running the Latin Kings. To Israel and Fabian, who shared their experiences of criminal life. And to Drusilla Lawton, who hosted us in her wonderful Park Slope apartment, and Illya Szilak and Chris Vroom, who extended their hospitality in Williamsburg, Brooklyn.

In London, we must thank Baillie Aaron, who generously shared with us her work to reintegrate ex-offenders into society. To the Point People, who provided constant friendship, leads for research, and moral support, particularly: Sarah Douglas, Cassie Robinson, Ella Saltmarshe, Anna Mouser, Hannah Smith, and Eleanor Ford. To the many hackers and computer scientists who shared their tales of genius and mischief, particularly Sam Roberts, Nathaniel Borenstein, and DM. To all of the fellow writers at Prufrock Coffee and Café Oberholz who commiserated with us during shared episodes of writers' block, as well as Asi Sharabi, who provided a desk to work from when it was needed. And finally, heartfelt and enormous gratitude must go to Fran Smith for her kind, wise, and compassionate guidance along the way.

A big thank-you to our Kickstarter backers who helped get this project off the ground—without a committed grassroots financing campaign, we never would have made it this far. To Laura Gamse, our talented filmmaker, who traveled with us to India and China and whose father diligently emailed us misfit material throughout the journey. To the community of staff and fellows at Ashoka with whom we connected around the world. And to members of the One/Thousand network, who supported us throughout this entire journey.

Thanks to Nathan Schneider for sharing his reflections on the Occupy movement and to Peter Leeson and Marcus Rediker, who spoke to us about the history of pirates. Thank you to David Kyuman Kim and Ken Knisely, early philosophical influences. Thanks to Marvin Gaye Chetwynd for opening our eyes to the world of performance art, to Will Bueche for his guidance and feedback on Dr. John Mack's study of alien abduction, and to Gary Slutkin for the incredible work he is doing to cure the world of violence. To Mark Hay, Yusuf Mohamed Hasan, and Jay Bahadur, who provided guidance with our story on Somali pirates, and to Walid Abdul-Wahab, Alicia

Sully, Philippa Young, and Sebastian Lindstrom for speaking to us about camel milk often over the years. To Jon Lackman and Lazar Kunstmann, for speaking to us about the UX and its infectious culture, and to Gaspard Duval, who took us thirty-five meters below Paris. To the talented illustrators and graphic designers Tom Jennings, Scott Roberts, Harry Mylonadis, and Bernard Myburgh for giving *The Misfit Economy* a beautiful visual identity. And to Paul Hyde Mezier, Fereshteh Amarsi, Mohamed Ali, Margaux Pelen, and Laurent Billiers for their valuable help with various translations.

Thanks for the love and support of our friends, particularly Zach Verdin, Charlotte Saunders, Maricarmen Sierra, Lily Bernheimer, Krista Knight, Alice Shay, Elizabeth Sperber, Alexis Smagula, Freya Zaheer, Pedro Jardim, Antonin Léonard, Tomás de Lara, Jake Levitas, Rachel West, Adam Sobolew, Jolie Olivetti, Gwen Bueno de Mesquita, Ilana Savdie, Katie Tsouros, Sasha de Marigny, Tara Yip-Bannicq, Darren Ryan, William McQuillan, Samantha Prada, Natalie Chesler, Leyla Sacks, Nico Luchsinger, Eva Mohr, Tahnee Prior, Amanda Gore, and many, many others—too many to list—in Sydney, Dublin, Berlin, Nairobi, London, and New York.

Thank you to the cities of London and Berlin for providing incredible creative and inspiring refuges to work on iterations of this manuscript and being magnets for underground and disruptive cultures.

Finally, immeasurable gratitude and love must go to our families, who provided a constant stream of love, support, and encouragement. This book would not have been possible without you.

NOTES

INTRODUCTION

1. Charles Passy, "At $18 a Pint, Camel's Milk May Make You Healthy, Poor," Market Watch, June 14, 2014, http://www .marketwatch.com/story/got-camel-milk-2014-06-13?dist =beforebell.
2. Jeanine Bentley, "Trends in U.S. Per Capita Consumption of Dairy Products, 1970–2012," United States Department of Agriculture, June 2, 2014, http://www.ers.usda.gov/amber-waves /2014-june/trends-in-us-per-capita-consumption-of-dairy -products,-1970-2012.aspx#.U94KUYBdWwG.
3. *The Oxford English Dictionary* (Oxford: Oxford University Press, May 10, 2012).
4. Interpol, United Nations Office on Drug and Crime, World Bank, "Pirate Trails: Tracking the Illicit Financial Flows from

Pirate Activities off the Horn of Africa," The World Bank, November 4, 2013.
5. Ibid.

1. THE MISFIT PHILOSOPHY

1. Jon Lackman, "The New French Hacker-Artist Underground," *Wired*, January 20, 2012, http://www.wired.com/2012/01/ff_ux/all/.
2. Barbara Evans, *Freedom to Choose: The Life and Work of Dr. Helena Wright, Pioneer of Contraception* (London: Bodley Head, 1984).
3. Roshan Paul and Alexa Clay, "An Open Source Approach to Medical Research," *Stanford Social Innovation Review*, October 3, 2011.
4. "The World's Billionaires," *Forbes*, http://www.forbes.com/profile/richard-branson/.
5. Steve Daniels, "Thai Hackers Adapt Vehicles and Buildings to the Flood," *Atlantic*, November 14, 2011, http://www.theatlantic.com/technology/archive/2011/11/thai-hackers-adapt-vehicles-and-buildings-to-the-flood/248467/#slide3.
6. *Economist*, "In Praise of Misfits," June 2, 2012, http://www.economist.com/node/21556230.
7. Shirley S. Wang, "How Autism Can Help You Land a Job," *Wall Street Journal*, March 27, 2014, http://online.wsj.com/news/articles/SB10001424052702304418404579465561364868556.
8. "The HOW Report: New Metrics for a New Reality: Rethinking the Source of Resiliency, Innovation, and Growth," LRN, 2012, http://pages.lrn.com/how-report.
9. Jared Duval, *Next Generation Democracy: What the Open Source Revolution Means for Power, Politics and Change* (New York: Bloomsbury, 2010).
10. Kim Gittleson, "Can a Company Live Forever?" BBC News, January 19, 2012, http://www.bbc.co.uk/news/business-16611040.

2. HUSTLE

1. Matthew C. Sonfield and Robert J. Barbato, "Testing Prison Inmates for Entrepreneurial Aptitude," May 19, 2004, Hofstra University and Rochester Institute of Technology.
2. Linda Anderson, "Troubled Teenagers Equal Entrepreneurial Success," *Financial Times*, March 18, 2013, http://www.ft.com /cms/s/2/a8c08352-8c9b-11e2-aed2-00144feabdc0.html #axzz3IrN7GYCD.
3. Peter Wagner and Leah Sakala, "Mass Incarceration: The Whole Pie," *Prison Policy Initiative*, March 12, 2014, http://www .prisonpolicy.org/reports/pie.html.
4. Matthew C. Sonfield, "From Inmate to Entrepreneur: A Preliminary Analysis," Hofstra University.
5. Raphael Minder, "In Spain, Jobless Find a Refuge Off the Books," *New York Times*, May 16, 2012, http://www.nytimes .com/2012/05/17/world/europe/spaniards-go-underground -to-fight-slump.html?pagewanted=all&_r=0.
6. Benedict Dellot, "Untapped Enterprise: Living with the Informal Economy," The Royal Society of Arts, September 2012, https://www.thersa.org/globalassets/pdfs/blogs/enterprise -untapped_enterprise-rsa.pdf.
7. Ibid.
8. Vivian Giang, "40 Percent of Americans Will Be Freelancers by 2020," *Business Insider*, March 21, 2013.
9. "CBS News Profiles HERO's Pam Dorr," Impact Design Hub, September 10, 2013, http://www.impactdesignhub.org/2013/09 /10/cbs-news-profiles-heros-pam-dorr-2/.

3. COPY

1. "2013 Passenger Vehicle Sales by Brand," ChinaAuto Web: A Guide to China's Auto Industry, January 15, 2014, http://

chinaautoweb.com/2014/01/2013-passenger-vehicle-sales-by
-brand/.

2. Peter Andreas, "Piracy and Fraud Propelled the U.S. Industrial Revolution," Bloomberg, February 1, 2013, http://www.bloom berg.com/news/2013-02-01/piracy-and-fraud-propelled-the -u-s-industrial-revolution.html.

3. Stephen Mihm, "A Nation of Outlaws: A Century Ago, That Wasn't China—It Was Us," *Boston Globe*, August 26, 2007, http://www.boston.com/news/globe/ideas/articles/2007/08/26 /a_nation_of_outlaws/?page=full.

4. "Knock-offs Catch On," *Economist*, March 4, 2010, http://www .economist.com/node/15610089.

5. "Chinese Authorities Find 22 Fake Apple Stores," BBC News, August 12, 2011, http://www.bbc.co.uk/news/technology-1450 3724.

6. Julie Zaveloff and Robert Johnson, "China Unveils a Knockoff Version of an Entire Austrian Village," *Business Insider*, June 4, 2012, http://www.businessinsider.com/china-has-built-a-copy cat-version-of-an-entire-austrian-village-2012-6.

7. Robin Wauters, "Investors Pump $90 Million into Airbnb Clone Wimdu," Techcrunch, June 14, 2011, http://techcrunch .com/2011/06/14/investors-pump-90-million-into-airbnb -clone-wimdu/.

8. Matt Cowan, "Inside the Clone Factory: The Story of Germany's Samwer Brothers," *Wired*, March 2, 2012, http://www .wired.co.uk/magazine/archive/2012/04/features/inside-the -clone-factory/viewall.

9. Oded Shenkar, *Copycats: How Smart Companies Use Imitation to Gain a Strategic Edge* (Boston: Harvard Business Review Press, 2010).

10. Steven Johnson, *Where Good Ideas Come From: The Seven Patterns of Innovation* (New York: Penguin, 2011).

11. John H. Lienhard, "Engines of Our Ingenuity," Episode 357,

University of Houston, 1989, http://www.uh.edu/engines/epi 357.htm/.

12. Robert Allen, "Collective Invention," *Journal of Economic Behavior and Organization* 4 (1983): 1–24.

13. Ibid.

14. Charles Leadbeater, *We-Think* (London: Profile Books, 2009).

15. Gregory Ferenstein, "Mark Cuban's Awesome Justification for Endowing a Chair to 'Eliminate Stupid Patents,'" Techcrunch, January 31, 2013, http://techcrunch.com/2013/01/31/mark -cubans-awesome-justification-for-endowing-a-chair-for-eli minating-stupid-patents/.

16. "20 Years of IBM Patents," IBM, http://www.research.ibm.com /articles/patents.shtml.

17. Robert Atkinson. "In Praise of Big Business," Innovation Files, June 22, 2012, http://www.innovationfiles.org/in-praise-of-big -business-part-1/.

18. Ronald Riley, "American Patent System About to Be Crippled," R. R. Enterprises, Inc., last revised November 21, 2001, http:// www.rjriley.com/multinationals/.

19. Michele Boldrin and David K. Levine, "The Case Against Patents," *Journal of Economic Perspectives* 27, no. 1 (Winter 2013): 3–22.

20. Select Committee on Patents, Parliament Papers, xviii, 1851, p. 812.

21. Zorina Khan, "An Economic History of Patent Institutions." Published online by the Economic History Association, http:// eh.net/encyclopedia/an-economic-history-of-patent-institutions/.

22. Yolanda Tayler, ed., *Battling HIV/AIDS: A Decision Maker's Guide to the Procurement of Medicines and Related Supplies*. The World Bank, 2004, p. 80.

23. D. B. Greco and M. Simão, "Brazilian Policy of Universal Access to AIDS Treatment: Sustainability Challenges and Perspectives." *AIDS 2007* 21 (suppl 4): S37–45.

24. "Brazil Requests Voluntary Licensing for AIDS Drugs to Treat

More Patients, Reduce Costs of Importing Patented Drugs," Kaiser Health News, March 17, 2005, http://www.medicalnews today.com/medicalnews.php?newsid=21378.

25. Toshiko Takenaka, *Patent Law and Theory* (Northampton, MA: Edward Elgar Publishing, 2009) 129.

26. Tim Westergren, "Pandora and Artist Payments," Pandora Blog, October 9, 2012, http://blog.pandora.com/2012/10/09 /pandora-and-artist-payments/.

27. Daniel Ek, "Two Billion and Counting," Spotify Artists, November 12, 2014, http://www.spotifyartists.com/2-billion-and -counting/.

28. Mike Hopkins, "A Strong 2013," Hulu Blog, December 18, 2013, http://blog.hulu.com/2013/12/18/a-strong-2013/.

29. "Overview," Investor Relations, Netflix, April 7, 2015, http:// ir.netflix.com/.

30. Erica Orden, Christopher S. Stewart, and Ian Sherr, "Disney Deal Puts Netflix in Pay-TV Big League," *Wall Street Journal*, December 4, 2012, http://online.wsj.com/articles/SB10001424 127887323901604578159432752905010.

31. Joost Schellevis, "Netflix baseert aanbod deels op populariteit video's op piraterijsites," September 14, 2013, http://tweakers .net/nieuws/91282/netflix-baseert-aanbod-deels-op-populari teit-videos-op-piraterijsites.html.

32. Steven Johnson, *Where Good Ideas Come From: The Seven Patterns of Innovation* (New York: Penguin, 2011).

33. Part of this text appears in an article written by Alexa Clay and Roshan Paul titled "Scaling Social Impact by Giving Away Value," which appeared in the *Stanford Social Innovation Review* on September 26, 2011, http://www.ssireview.org/blog/entry /scaling_social_impact_by_giving_away_value.

34. Kurt Wagner, "Facebook Has a Quarter of a Trillion User Photos," Mashable, September 17, 2013, http://mashable.com /2013/09/16/facebook-photo-uploads/.

4. HACK

1. Gabriella Coleman, "Our Weirdness Is Free," Triple Canopy, http://canopycanopycanopy.com/contents/our_weirdness_is_free.
2. Aaron Swartz, "Guerilla Open Access Manifesto," July 2008, https://archive.org/details/GuerillaOpenAccessManifesto.
3. Official statement from family and partner of Aaron Swartz, http://www.rememberaaronsw.com/memories/.
4. Richard Flanders, *If a Pirate I Must Be . . . : The True Story of Bartholomew Roberts—King of the Caribbean* (London: Aurum Press, 2008).
5. Peter T. Leeson, *The Invisible Hook: The Hidden Economics of Pirates* (Princeton, NJ: Princeton University Press, 2011).
6. Marcus Rediker, *Villains of All Nations: Atlantic Pirates in the Golden Age* (Boston: Beacon Press, 2005).
7. Ibid.
8. Charles Johnson, *A General History of the Robberies and Murders of the Most Notorious Pirates* (Conway Maritime Press, 2002).
9. Leeson, *The Invisible Hook*.
10. Ibid.
11. Rediker, *Villains of All Nations*.
12. Johnson, *A General History of the Robberies and Murders of the Most Notorious Pirates*.
13. Leeson, *The Invisible Hook*.
14. Rediker, *Villains of All Nations*.
15. Ibid.
16. Epicenter Staff, "Mark Zuckerberg's Letter to Investors: 'The Hacker Way,'" *Wired*, February 1, 2012, http://www.wired.com/2012/02/zuck-letter/.
17. Ivan Arreguín-Toft, "How the Weak Win Wars: A Theory of Asymmetric Conflict," *International Security* 26, no. 1 (Summer 2001): 93–128.

18. Moises Naim, *Illicit: How Smugglers, Traffickers, and Copycats Are Hijacking the Global Economy* (London: Arrow, 2007).
19. Ibid.
20. Marc Goodman, "What Business Can Learn from Organized Crime," *Harvard Business Review*, November 2011, https://hbr.org/2011/11/what-business-can-learn-from-organized-crime/ar/1.
21. Jon Lackman, "The New French Hacker-Artist Underground," *Wired*, January 20, 2012, http://www.wired.com/2012/01/ff_ux/all/.

6. PIVOT

1. *Black and Gold: The Story of the Almighty Latin King and Queen Nation*, Big Noise Films, May 19, 2009.
2. "N.J. Homicides Soared to Seven-Year High in 2013 After Surges in Newark, Trenton," on www.nj.com/news, January 1, 2014.
3. Parts of this story first appeared in Alexa Clay, "Growing Up Alien," in *Aeon*, January 17, 2014.
4. John Mack interviewed by Jeffrey Mishlove for the TV program *Thinking Allowed* (1994).
5. John Mack interviewed by Roméo DiBenedetto, M.Div, on the cable TV program *Emerging Renaissance*, in 1997.
6. John Mack interviewed by Russell E. DiCarlo, 1994. Published in: Russell DiCarlo, ed., *Towards a New World View: Conversations at the Leading Edge* (Erie, PA: Epic Publishing, 1995) 303–312.

7. WALKING THE MISFIT PATH

1. Dov Seidman, "Rethinking Occupy Wall Street," *Forbes*, October 21, 2011, http://www.forbes.com/sites/dovseidman/2011/10/21/rethinking-occupy-wall-street/.

INDEX

INDEX